PARTISAN POLITICS

The Errors of Our Heroes Past 3

Examining the Political Intrigues & Election Outcomes in the Giant of Africa

CHRIS LEO
The Thinking Mind

TABLE OF CONTENTS

INTRODUCTION

Politics, they say, is a dirty game that only the dirty ones can play. The political landscape has been in deep contentions and confusion from the very beginning. Over the centuries, great men and women have continued to research on ways to arrest the unhealthy developments around the political institution. The manners and methods, the strategies and skills, the plots and patterns of engagement by these people have been mind-blowing in perspective, but the success they have recorded has been quite disappointing. One thing has been missing – the basic understanding of the central and core ingredient for human success, the GOD-factor!

God is sovereign; He rules, and cannot be ruled out of the system. Whether we acknowledge this or not does not change it from being the truth. Instead, our lack of this basic understanding that God has been at the centre of our existence has given birth to a self-styled approach to facing great challenges before us. It has also made some of us either ignorant or defiant of the right way. Hence, in our self-styled approach to winning, thus neglecting the WAY of God, we end up with a fat harvest of errors!

As we enter a more critical stage of our national life where the realities of our present world pitch against our core values as a people, staring us in the face, we must begin to count our teeth with our tongues. For us to begin to enjoy the dividend of the earth which the Almighty God has freely given us, we must, as a matter of essence, begin to consolidate on some of the already established structures and platforms for national progress and unity as affirmed by the Council of Heaven. We must also repair the ones that have been in serious deteriorating conditions. And for us to repair and consolidate, we must carefully and traditionally probe the past to identify the factors that have brought us either the little success we have enjoyed or the mass failure that we have bemoaned. Then looking into our seemingly awful past will lead us to discover those things that contributed to our national gains and interest as well as those that drew us into retrogression and regrets. This is the crux of this timely series, **The Errors of Our Heroes Past.**

The Holy Bible is full of examples of political leadership that went contrary to their original design. PARTISAN POLITICS – the third volume in the series, The Errors of our Heroes Past, is an approach for us discover why the Nigerian state has been staggering in political instability even with the involvement of intelligent minds. In it, you will find:

❖ The foolishness of trying to solve national challenges by sensual wisdom alone

* The error of copying negative attributes of other nations
* How kingdoms are lost and kings are replaced
* Why human leadership that does not align with Heaven ends in anarchy, and
* What made partisan politics incapable of solving our national needs

PARTISAN POLITICS gives a thorough outlook on some of the people who brought us seeming freedom, but did not understand the demands of freedom or the workings of an independent state. It unveils the challenges these leaders faced and their responses to those challenges, and how their responses affected their generations, and have continued to affect generations after them till date. It provides the window to view, from God's perspective, the actions of those men (and women), heroes in their own right; what must be learnt and what must be avoided so that our contemporary existence can be more blessed than bruised.

This book does not in any way 'challenge' or 'question' statutory or ordained authorities but it throws a challenge to those who either by divine privilege or people's mandate find themselves in the saddle of leadership, to learn from their past counterparts at all levels – learning from their foolishness not to be foolish, and from their wisdom to be wiser. By so doing, we all and our progeny will be far from repeating the errors of our heroes past.

Chris Leo Nwachukwu
January 2011

CHAPTER ONE

THE PEOPLE'S CHOICE

Introducing...

The physical height of a man usually gives the impression that he is mature in mind and body. It sometimes tells if one had come of age or not. It is oftentimes a strong determinant of how others see and respond to him.

But the physical height of a man does not determine his height of ideas, height of maturity, or his spiritual altitude. The facial or outward beauty of one is not even an indication that they are beautiful inside. It could just be an artificial complexion that has no inward bearing.

Hence the choice of a national leader or a leader at any level should not be based on artificial beauty or outward qualities but of the beauty that stems from the inside.

Besides being the favourite son of an influential man from the smallest tribe in Israel, he was the most handsome man; not only in the tribe of Benjamin, but in all Israel at that time. Saul was the son of a great political stalwart named Kish from the tribe of Benjamin.

<h1 style="text-align:center"><u>The Old Corrupt Order</u></h1>

The Holy Bible said that Saul was head and shoulders taller than anyone else in the land! (1 Samuel 9 TLB) His emergence as the first head of state and commander in chief of his country – anointed and sworn-in by God's prophet, Samuel, followed a sequence of dramatic events in the history of his country.

First, the nation's high priest Eli, who was supposed to provide proper legislation for the people of his country, had failed in his assignment. He also failed in the proper discipline of his children who should have succeeded him in the Aaronic priesthood as enshrined in the constitution of their country. As a result, the entire country lived in error, thus attracted divine sentence with the invading of their land by the mighty Philistines – the cursed descendants of Noah; people who refused to be slaves to any nation.

Second was the invasion by the Philistines which led to the deaths of Eli the high priest, his two legislator-sons, Hophni and Phinehas who would have succeeded him if they had lived right, and also the death of Phinehas' wife who was just delivered of a baby boy they named Ichabod. Ichabod means "glory is gone or departed" from the land. These were the second and third tragedies.

The first tragedy was the capture of the ark of God by the no-retreat, no-surrender, resilient, and hard-fighting Philistines, but the Ark was later deported to the hillside home of Abinadab whose son Eleazar took charge of it for 20 years. The Ark of God was a sign of good omen for the country and it represented the presence of God with them. Then, the Holy Bible records,

"...and during that time all Israel was in sorrow because the Lord had seemingly abandoned them" (7 vs. 2 TLB)

Then, Eli's boy and apprentice-priest Samuel had become a well-known prophet whose words were not to be trifled with. Samuel became their judge. He was, in fact, the number one prophet in God's Executive and Legislative Council. He launched revival, re-orientation and re-branding campaigns all over the country until age was no longer in his favor. Our bible history records,

"In his old age, Samuel retired and appointed his sons as judges in his place...but they were not like their father, for they were greedy for money. They accepted bribes and were very corrupt in the administration of justice" (8 vs. 1-3 TLB)

Please permit a very necessary digression at this juncture. Although we are talking about Saul Kish of Benjamin, yet we cannot afford to overlook the error that emanated from the family of the nation's number one holy man; an error that has, through the years, ravaged and damaged the image of our own sacred judicial institution.

A look at the history of our country's judicial system would reveal that these errors are not new. A former Chief Justice of Nigeria, Justice Dahiru Musdapher once said in Abuja: **"I feel it is honorable to admit that things are not as they ought to be."**

He also admitted and submitted that **"...there is no disputing the fact that as it stands today, it appears that the society we serve is not entirely satisfied with our performance".** The later he said while addressing a forum at the Nigerian Institute of Advanced Legal Studies (NIALS).

No doubt, as it was with the sons of Eli the chief judge and high priest and the sons of Samuel the chief judge, prophet and member of God's Executive Council, so it has been with so many of our so-called learned fellows in our dear land. Very unfortunate, I would say.

The following comments corroborate what I am talking about:

"There are indications either from comments made by the public or from personal experience that there is a need to be concerned about the lowering of standards in the judiciary of this country. It was once thought to be only in the magistracy because of the disturbing

way some of the personnel tended to abuse their office. It gradually crawled to the high courts and would appear to have had a foothold among noticeable number of judicial officers there. There is the aspect of their attitude and orientation to duty; late sitting, laziness, incompetence, doubtful integrity, impertinence towards counsel."

(Justice Samson Uwaifo, Supreme Court Jurist, 2006)

"There are known instances where recommendations are not made on the merits but on the grounds of favoritism and nepotism. Some candidates go about campaigning for appointments as judges and they do so shamelessly."   (Justice Niki Tobi, Supreme Court Jurist, 1999 rtd)

Samuel, though a good man, yet, had corrupt children whom he thought were good to go with the leadership of the nation and the administration of justice. But he was wrong.

Similarly we have had leaders in our dear country and the continent of Africa who had wanted their own children, friends, family members, or close associates and loyalists to succeed them upon their retirement. Some of these leaders were good while others were very corrupt and wicked.

More often than not, the good and righteous ones who probably wanted their children or their people to take over from them were probably convinced of their maturity, loyalty to God, and their dedication to their fatherland before making such decisions. But again, they were wrong, and their decisions and moves had severally met with stiff rejection and opposition by other leaders of thought who felt that the leadership of a nation or an entity should not be a family or association business.

Those who ruined their countries and had wanted their children to take over from them had ulterior motives and hidden agenda. One of their fears was that an outsider could launch investigation into their past and hunt them down should skeletons be found in their cupboards.

Someone like the late Muammar Gaddafi of Libya is an example of African despots whose children wanted to succeed but for the disapproval of their people, and the UN with its allied forces.

Unlike the case of Samuel, it was Gaddafi's sons that requested a cease-fire by NATO forces on their corrupt father in order for them to take over the leadership of their country. A case where the goat's head still goes into the goat's bag!

Prophet Samuel's case reminds us of the repeated cases of failure of quality parenting and guidance by several leaders all over the African continent.

If we take a journey down memory lane, we would hardly recall cases where the posterity and progeny of most of our past leaders were involved or committed to the development of the nation and in the proper administration of justice in our country. Few of them only made a brief appearance on the stage of national leadership either in the polity or the economy, but none had really taken the principal character in our national life.

Of course, except Donald Duke of Cross River state and a few others whose contributions to the Nigerian state in diverse ways speak volume of their ancestral consistency in national concerns, others had been in the opposite.

The Otedolas and the Obasanjos have had their share in the economy and the polity respectively in the representation of Femi Otedola and Iyabo Obasanjo. However, these two had been involved in one allegation of corruption or misrepresentation of public trust or the other.

I know there are yet others whose antecedents had contributed enormously to the development of the Nigerian state but were never so popular like those already mentioned, and these had represented themselves and their rather unpopular ancestors very well. But a careful study at the greater number of men who had ruled this nation since independence will reveal that their progeny, like the children of Samuel, never lived up to expectation.

One had expected that the children of a man of integrity and positive influence should have towed the line of their father. We had also expected that the godly life of such men would have rubbed off on their children. But the opposite was the case in the life of Samuel and his children who he made judges in his place.

So also we had expected that the M.K.Os, the Awolowos, the Azikiwes, the Obasanjos, the IBBs, the Buharis, and many others would have had children who became national icons not only in politics, but in other spheres where they could shine as lights, correct the errors of their fathers, and surpass their few accomplishments in Nigeria and in Africa. Instead, disappointment had greeted the lot of us who had nursed that expectation.

We know that parents cannot fully control and determine how their children turn out, but they can give lots of energy, time, and other resources to their parenting, and most importantly, their lifestyle at home and away. While these may not guarantee that their children grow up perfect, it will definitely make a whole lot of difference in how much of their parents' faith and positive lifestyle they adopt and shape into their own.

The question now is: What kind of lifestyle and faith do you, a hero, see as positive that your children whom many are expecting to take over from you can adopt into their own life? What kind of life do you see as positive enough to be represented anywhere in the world? So many people do not see corruption as a big deal, and that is why their children take after them in it and the rest of the society quickly reject them.

Some of our leaders see governance as a do-or-die affair and so their children who do not subscribe to that kind of leadership lose interest in them, focus on their own interests, and even tend to live alone in their own world. Some others who had messed up their leadership grace forbid their children from going into public life so as not to tow the same line and perhaps end up victims.

But Prophet Samuel knew that it is possible to be in the public eye; in the public service, and yet keep a clean cupboard without skeletons. He tested it from childhood when he served under a myopic first class priest, Eli who could not properly discipline his greedy and corrupt children, and concluded that his own children would not fail. But he was wrong about his children; they failed. And that was the last instance that led to the emergence of Saul Kish as head of state and commander in chief of the armed forces of Israel. Our bible history records:

"Then all the elders of Israel gathered themselves together, and came to Samuel unto Ramah, and said unto him, Behold, thou art old, and thy sons walk not in thy ways: now make us a king to judge us like all the nations. But the thing displeased Samuel, when they said, Give us a king to judge us. And Samuel prayed unto the LORD" (8 vs. 4-6)

"Finally, the leaders of Israel met in Ramah to discuss the matter with Samuel. They told him that since his retirement things hadn't been the same, for his sons were not good men. 'Give us a king like all other nations have,' they pleaded. Samuel was terribly upset and went to the Lord for advice" (TLB)

Quest for Independence

God had been the King over His people and Samuel was just His spokesman. But because of the hard-heartedness of the people encouraged by the misbehavior of Samuel's two sons who had assumed office as his replacement, the people indirectly rejected God who was their Head of State and Commander in Chief. They wanted to be like other nations around them who had human commanders. This is the error of the followers inspired by the leaders.

While other nations had envied them because of their God who was always there for them all the time to fight their battles, the people of God themselves grew tired and unhappy. What was their problem anyway? Why would a nation under God rebel and seek to be under the imperfect leadership of mere mortals?

I have discovered that no matter how good a leader of a nation is, there are still people in that nation who would still not be happy with him for one reason or the other. No matter how promptly he delivers the good of the land and the good dividends of his leadership to them, they would have one reason or another for their unhappiness and dissatisfaction.

When the colonial masters were ruling Nigeria and other African countries, our fathers were not satisfied with the arrangement – strangers ruling the owners of the land. They came up with a million reasons why they should be their own masters and rule themselves. Finally, the colonial masters left our shores though they did not leave with their personal and corporate interests, and our people heaved a sigh of relief, but not for too long.

This is because our post-independence heroes who got the shackles of colonialism off our ankles and wrists soon forgot the importance of the unity of our existence and embarked on a wild goose chase. They began to entrench personal interests in the name of national interests. Then the generation that followed them **_"gathered themselves together"_** (political party formation) and called for different kinds of government they felt would establish the needed change and re-establish the estranged unity.

Even in recent times, in this 21st century; in the time of the much-desired democracy, some dissatisfied groups have kept calling for a gathering or a solemn assembly to discuss the best form of leadership for our country.

If Nigeria was a country like Israel of old under the leadership of God through an Enoch Adeboye, William Kumuyi, or any other single human instrument without a national assembly, federal executive council, a governors' forum, and a presidency, I bet there are people who would call for His resignation or outright impeachment by a non-authorized selected few. Of course a two-third majority would be useless. They would have also requested for another human leader, of course not an Enoch Adeboye or a William Kumuyi, but someone who would be there for them anytime on their terms.

But was God not there for the old Israel? Has God not been there for Nigeria? Has he not been there for Africa and the rest of the world? Truth is: God has been there.

He has not changed His address or residence – He is the Omnipresence.

The problem is that God has not been there for them on their terms. In fact, God will never be there for us on our terms. He was never there for Israel of old to manipulate, and will never be there for Nigeria or Africa or the rest of the world to manipulate.

The depraved nature of man incites him to always strive to take charge without any other bothering him with why this or why that. Human beings in the fallen nature, being earthy, desire and covet self-rule, and would even do anything to hijack it from their leaders or rulers. That was what Israel did. It has also happened in this country and in some other African states.

To some of them, the divine leadership of God was not profiting them well. To them, God was not there to answer their numerous rhetorical questions. He was not there physically so they could engage Him in their political debates and diplomatic rigmarole like they did to their human leaders afterwards.

Because humans do not see God in His physical appearance or form, they find it impossible to properly relate to Him. Not because they cannot relate, but because they have limited themselves to a no-faith life which contrasts the God-life. The Word of God says that the just shall live by faith; that anyone who comes to

God must first believe He is, and that without faith, it is impossible to please God.

Human beings want someone they can harass and intimidate to do their bidding and run errands for them. And since God is not available for that because He is not like that, they give Him a vote of no confidence. They want a king or a president or a leader who must listen to their ranting whether they make sense or not, and they expect him to respond promptly.

They want a leader whose palace or office they can barge into to demand explanations on why some policies and regulations do not work in their favor. They would want to know why their requisitions and petitions do not get preferential and urgent treatment; why their family members, friends, or party loyalists and officials do not get appointed on the cabinet or other special committees.

In our clime, these people would want God to explain why He should allow some people, like the sons of Samuel who mismanaged and abused their mandates, to still stay alive. We would have seen even some clergy and politicians stage protests to the office of God demanding full explanation why some of their "weak" counterparts should still be holding their offices. And you can guess what the scenario would have been like if these things had happened in the time of old – a time of the law of sin and death. Many of the protesters would not have lived to tell their story or share their experience. Thank God for grace. Yet, people question God over some issues and they are still alive.

For Israel, other nations around them had kings and presidents who led them to battles even though they severally lost and some killed in the battles. Those nations had no God of the Angel Armies, but gods they could put anywhere, handle anyhow, and discard anytime they failed them. Israel had seen how other kings boasted of their military might and valor anytime the battle with them was set.

But for Israel, no one to parade himself and boast as their champion too except for the prophet or priest who gave them divine directions concerning the battle. For them, God who was their King and Commander in Chief would come whenever He decided was the right time to show up even though He never arrived late at any scene of their battles.

Even though they had always enjoyed the victories God got for them in the end, they were yet not satisfied with the arrangement. Even though they had always bowed in awe and reverence, and worshipped God for the victory, yet some of them wanted things the other way round – they were not always happy with God's timing. It was often at the peak of their anxiety and fear of being defeated at war that God usually showed up. That timing, to them, was not okay.

They must have recalled the poignant memories of those episodes where the Egyptians almost caught up with them at the Red Sea; the Midianite invasion of their territory; and later the Philistine assault on their country from the days of their forefathers. They must have thought of how they yelled, wept, and cried before God stepped in and delivered them. All these and probably more must have made them to ask for a human leader whose response they could predict, and who would lead them in battle like other nations.

Perhaps, they would not have to be apprehensive of any defeat if their commander in chief were a brave man, neither would they fear nor tremble at the boasting of the champions of their enemies since theirs would be there from the start. At least, having a king to go before them could save them of the moments of heightened anxiety that they severally experienced in the past waiting on God to arrive at the scene. However, they failed to understand how God works from generation to generation.

Our country is much like Israel of Bible times. When it's well with us, we praise God but when it goes wrong, God gets a red card. Furthermore, when the colonial masters left us to rule ourselves, our heroes sang the

"Redemption Song". Then things went bad and they, like the Israelites, began to sing "By the Rivers of Babylon". They then asked the military to intervene and put things in order. After several years, the military option did not favor them, and then they began to sing "Mr. Jailer" and "Fire on the Mountain".

Suddenly, there was a stepping aside, and subsequently, a permanent stepping out of the Aso Rock by the junta, and Mr. Democracy stepped in. Soon, they began to be weary of the first democratic government and so began to sing other different songs.

When the late President Umaru Yar'Adua came in, they said that the king that would lead us to battle against the number one enemy of our progress, Mr. Corruption, had emerged with Goodluck as his helper. Not quite long, death did them part, but Goodluck survived.

Then the same band of elders joined by their newly groomed democrats of the younger generation began to sing aloud that the Messiah had arrived finally. All the while, God was side-lined and was only carried along when necessary – yes, when they felt necessary. That's why human government divided this world into secular and sacred: one controlled by themselves and the other by God. But it was not so from the beginning of creation!

But just recently, the oil subsidy palaver prompted some of those people to think otherwise; that the messiah may not have emerged after all. That, you know, reminds me of a literature book we read at school, "The Beautiful Ones Are Not Yet Born".

When human beings feel that God is late while He has taking His time to groom them into a faith-life and, in His infinite mercy, is giving them the opportunity to be strong and solid in their relationship with Him, they conclude that God has failed his promise. But the Word of God has this to say to such fellows:

"God is it not late with his promises as some measure lateness. He is restraining himself on account of you, holding back the End because he doesn't want anyone lost. He has giving everyone space and time to change" (I Peter 3 vs. 9 TM)

So since our heroes did not see and understand how God works, they requested for a king who would lead them like other nations.

Now understand a point here. They did not ask for a leader who would deliver the dividends of governance to them. They did not ask for a leader who would show them the way to serve God better so that they could enjoy His numerous blessings. God's people did not even ask for a leader who would deliver them from the oppression of their enemies so they would not have to fight battles anymore. All that their myopic consciousness and depraved minds could inspire them to ask for was a king who would judge them, go before them, and fight their battles (8:20). You can imagine their request.

When a nation loses track of righteousness, it becomes tense and apprehensive of problems and threats that might never come. When I say "a nation", I am talking about the people there. But it is not all the people so to speak; just a group of people who believe they know what is good for their country and what their country needs at every point in time. Meanwhile, they forget that they are largely limited in ideas and knowledge, and that God is the Unlimited One who knows us better than we know ourselves. And their request displeased the chief spokesman of the Incumbent.

By asking for a leader that would fight their battles, they ungratefully failed to acknowledge and reverence the Incumbent God-of-the-Angel-Armies as their Commander in Chief, and Samuel as their National Security Adviser. They also, with that request for a king, succeeded in calling for and opening their borders to wars while locking God and Samuel out. What an error? And how did the Incumbent handle them? He told Samuel to listen to them and make them another ruler.

Now, for our contemporary heroes, here is a piece of wisdom. Samuel did not take it out with them; he let God decide. Samuel was not upset because they rejected him and his two corrupt sons, Joel and Abiah, like our politicians and their parents, godfathers, and sponsors would do when the people reject them or their nominees for political offices in the country. He was upset because they rejected God's ordinance and their sovereign constitution.

"But the thing displeased Samuel, when they said, Give us a king to judge us. And Samuel prayed unto the LORD (he asked God for advice)" Emphasis added

Samuel was not a leader that imposed himself on the people of his country. Remember how he started – as a child under Eli the priest. He was never an impostor and never played politics with his office as a prophet and judge. It was the ordinance of God that brought him to the stage of national leadership and service, and that ordinance the people rejected. He was their judge according to God's ordinance and not according to human election.

Unlike some of our contemporary heroes, Samuel did not become a national leader by popular votes, parliamentary decision or bureaucratic process, but by the enactment of a divine bill vetoed by the Council of

Heaven. Therefore, he was not displeased that his people had voted him out like some of our own leaders would do, but that they had cast a slight on God who was truly their leader and king. He did not start throwing his spiritual weight around as a prophet nor did he initiate diplomatic moves as the one in charge of the judicial system to get some of those elders to drop their request for another leader.

If some of our leaders on this global divide found themselves in Samuel's shoes, they would do everything in their tiny power to get at the people who led that delegation to Ramah. The ones who pretend to be civil could approach the law courts and pray them to quash such a suit, arguing that they already had a king and that they were his spokespersons. And if the courts failed to answer their "prayers" and upheld the suit, then they could adopt the doctrine of necessity which might include jungle justice or do-or-die politics to settle the matter out of court.

It might be true that the people, in requesting for a king while the Incumbent was still in charge, implied a rejection or violation of established ordinance. However, responding or reacting to it in the manner that I just illustrated above would also imply a violation of the same ordinance.

Whenever a people or their leaders reject the ordinance of God, they consequentially invite the will of the enemy. That was why God told Samuel not to be angry or displeased because they did not reject him but Him. Many years later, Prophet Isaiah after brooding over and analyzing the foolishness of his people, came up and declared,

"For the LORD is our judge, the LORD is our lawgiver, the LORD is our king; he will save us" (Chap. 33 vs. 22)

But his people, perhaps the elite class or the political stalwarts had said,

"...Nay; but we will have a king over us; that we also may be like all the nations, and that our king may judge us, and go out before us, and fight our battles"
(8 vs. 19-20)

These people understood the arms of government and their functions so they were not just ordinary folks; they're learned. Isaiah prophetically declared God as the Judge (Judiciary), the Lawgiver (Legislature), and the King (Presidency or Executive) of their country and of the whole world, and added that ***"he will save us"***. That means God is the ultimate government any country should have for He has able to save and will save them.

But these people had said, ***"Nay...we will have a king*** (government) ***over us...that our king*** (government) ***may*** *judge us* (litigate or arbitrate for us)*, and go out before us* (be our representative)*, and fight our battles* (be our executor or execute justice for us)"*.* Emphasis mine

By this request, they furthermore implied they wanted an amendment of the ordinance of God provided in their constitution – the Law of Moses, which made God their King and Sovereign Leader, the King of kings.

Remember that the senior citizens, the elite class, leaders of thought, and the political heavyweights had met and resolved what they felt was the best type of government for their country. They had resolved that their constitution, which was first written with the finger of God, and re-written by their first "post-independence" leader Moses within a forty-year transition, should be amended within a twinkle of an eye just because they wanted to be like other nations around. But they did not know that even in our time, the amendment of a law cannot be carried out by a resolution but by another law. It is not the case of *"the I's have it"* we often hear during sittings or plenaries in our national assembly. It needs to go through a process – the rule of law! So it was their error.

But come to think of it again: why exactly did they request for a human government? Why did they ask for the type of government that we have in our country that has never worked out our earnest desire? It is clear:

they wanted to be like other nations. They knew what they wanted but did not know the implication of that.

Oftentimes, our supposedly sincere aspirations contrast the perfect will of God for our lives. In a quest to achieve what we see or believe other people have achieved, we desire and work to be like them. We copy and imitate their style of living to our detriment, and in the process, we offend God seriously. Our desire must align with God-ordained purposes for our lives.

Although we are free to choose how to live; how to run our world and govern our people, yet our freedom to choose must be with responsibility to God first. Any choice that does not promote the will of God for a nation is first ungodly, and then, it is detrimental to that nation's unity and instrumental to its jeopardy and disintegration. We are not the Egyptians, the Philistines, or the Assyrians. We are not the Amalekites, the Corinthians, or any other people. We are Nigerians! We are God's own people!

Every country or race has their own peculiar environmental and structural challenges. They have what works for and against them. Their peoples are different from one another. Although there is nothing wrong in emulating other nations that are economically and politically doing well, yet every nation must study their history to find out what has worked and how it worked and whether those who first initiated it got their idea and backing from God or not. Moreover, aims and objectives must be clearly defined, terms and conditions must apply.

Israel of old depended on God-of-the-Angel-Armies and they overly enjoyed His protection and provisions. Other nations around them that they sought to become like never had the God-of-the-Angel-Armies, and they overly lived in darkness and doom. So that import – trying to be like those nations – was totally detrimental.

Suffice it to say that it is the duty of the leaders of the people to always seek Heaven's backing before embarking on anything. The whole essence of this present earth stemmed from the extension of God's rule to the world of man.

This Earth exists for one major purpose; that God might reign as the King of kings amongst men. That is why Jesus Christ taught us to pray, ***"Thy will be done in earth, as it is done in heaven"***. The will of God is that men will live freely under His divine rule as King – doing His will. His ultimate will is to have people who are loyal to Him – willing to submit themselves to Him; people He can relate to as family and joyfully call His own.

Israel was one fortunate nation, and I strongly believe Nigeria is another. But they had rejected God. They became like other nations without God or the nations that side-lined God and only referred to Him whenever they deemed necessary. It was on this sad premise – a manifestation of foolishness cum short-sightedness – that our main character in this book, Saul of Benjamin, emerged as the first anointed president and commander in chief of Israel.

Wrong Foundation

The first thing that was wrong with the choice of Saul as president of his country was his tribe. When Jacob blessed his sons shortly before he died in Egypt, he prophetically zoned the leadership of Israel to Judah. He did not mention that the presidency or kingship would be transferred to another tribe. Therefore, the presidency was zoned to Judah until Shiloh come (Genesis 49:10).

In fact, the issue of zoning of political offices did not start in Nigeria with Nigerians; it started in Egypt with Jacob and his descendants. It was Jacob who zoned the presidency to Judah just as he zoned the priesthood to the tribe of Levi.

Several years later in the time of the kings after the reign of Solomon, the once united kingdom was split into the northern and southern kingdoms of Israel and Judah respectively. And if you check the history of evil kings and bad presidents just for the records, they ruled Israel.

Ahab, for example, ruled Israel while Jehoshaphat was president over Judah. Jehoram, Nadab, Baasha, Zimri, Omri, Ahab, and thirteen others were all bad leaders that ruled that northern kingdom of Israel. None of them was good in the sight of God; they ended up like Saul in disobedience and like Jeroboam son of Nebat in idolatry.

But down south in Judah, presidents such as Asa, Jehoshaphat, Joash, Amaziah, Hezekiah, and Josiah were all godly men, good in the sight of God and men, and their reign was marked by the fear of God and total adherence to His commandment.

The point is that none of the leaders of the northern Israel had a good record except Jehu who carried out the commands of God in ridding the country of all Baal worshippers as well as destroying the dynasty of Ahab and Jezebel, the wicked president and his first lady respectively.

Why did they turn out bad and wicked and ineffective in their capacity as presidents? It was a result of the structure; an error that emanated from somewhere at a point in the history of the country. The Holy records had said, ***"The sceptre shall not depart from Judah, nor a lawgiver from between his feet, until Shiloh come"***. But the scepter did temporarily depart as ten tribes that made up the northern kingdom of Israel were ruled for centuries by presidents and governments from other tribes than Judah.

Meanwhile for David's sake and for the sake of God's name in Jerusalem, the rest tribes that made up the southern kingdom of Judah were ruled by presidents from the tribe of Judah. The scepter departed because the glory departed – Ichabod.

So, General Saul Kish emerged as the ruler of his country on a wrong foundation. It was a permissive arrangement due to the hard-heartedness of the people. It was a foundation erected on the rejection of the Almighty God as the Sovereign Ruler of the nation. A foundation built on a vote of no confidence in the Paramount Ruler of the Ends of the Earth. The Council of Heaven was not pleased with that development, and God foretold the people the kind of leadership they would get.

"Now therefore hearken unto their voice: howbeit yet protest solemnly unto them, and show them the manner of the king (government) *that shall reign over them...This will be the manner of the king that shall reign over you..."* Read I Samuel 8 vs. 9-18

There you will see the characteristics of the government that the Council of Heaven decided to give them in response to their request.

Another translation of that portion from our holy records puts it this way: ***"Do as they ask, but warn them about what it will be like to have a king!"*** (TLB). Yet another version***: "So let them have their way. But warn them of what they're in for. Tell them the way kings*** (human governments) ***operate, just what they're likely to get from a king*** (a human leader)" - TM, emphasis mine.

God said to Samuel to let them have their way – a very dangerous situation. God implied, "Since they have decided to govern themselves thereby rejecting me as their governor, let them go on with their decision. Soon they will realize the dire consequences of their error". They asked for a king – a human governor, a mortal president, and rejected the Governor amongst the nations, but they did not know what they were in for.

So God told His prophet to warn them. Yet, after the warning, they were bent on having an error-prone, weak-framed, and fallible earthly government instead of the infallible, ever-secure leadership of the Almighty God. ***"Nevertheless, the people refused to obey the voice of Samuel; and they said, Nay, but we will have a king over us".*** Mark one stubborn feature of the people of that country. It is disobedience – ***"The people refused to obey the voice..."***

So it was on this negative feature that Saul was made the president and commander in chief. His emergence was on the platform of the People's Disobedience to God Party (PDGP) – the prominent party in the whole land! I believe someone is seriously thinking right now.

There are no accidents in matters of destiny. History repeats itself. Saul's emergence on that platform gave a clue to political watchers and observers across the lands of what his government was likely going to become.

The People's Disobedience to God Party (PDGP) was a party of disobedient chieftains – democrats, perhaps. They wanted a "democracy" to replace the theocracy that had been on ground for centuries before they came to the scene, and God consented. They did not mind if that type of government was good for the overall interest of the country or bad enough to destroy them. They did not calculate very well if it was a solution well-tailored to address the challenges confronting the country at that material time, instead, all they wanted was to be like other nations.

At a seminar organized by the people of Ubulu-Uku, Delta State, Nigeria living in Lagos at Lagos Airport Hotel in 2008 which I moderated, the guest speaker Apostle (Prof) Joseph Mba said that solutions to any challenges or problems facing any entity must be tailored to suit and respond to those challenges.

Professor Joseph, the Director of Strategic Business School, Lagos, while delivering a paper on issues affecting our nation implied that the peculiarity of those challenges must be put into proper consideration before final decisions are reached on how best to tackle them. That is to say that all the sides must be looked at before arriving at the best approach to resolving issues. I believe this is what experts refer to as 'best practice'. But our heroes did not consult widely and wisely before jumping into conclusions and that had put our dear country in dicey situations at different times.

Even when Samuel, God's spokesman highlighted the features of that type of government, the people insisted on having their way. And because our God is not a coercive God that forces Himself or His ideals on mortals, He instructed Samuel to permissively give them their "independence" and to install a human president. And because that bill for a human government was not initiated by Heaven, and was not the original plan, the Council of Heaven decided that the president and commander in chief must not come from Judah. Yes, he must not come from the tribe that was prophetically zoned the presidency *"until Shiloh come"*.

Our Book has it that immediately there was an arrangement for their request to be granted – a permissive arrangement. The search began and Saul the son of Kish appeared on the scene.

Now, let us not cruise on with history and miss an important point here: an amazing character of God, which we are implored to learn. Even though the people had practically but ignorantly rejected God, yet God did not abandon them. He did not say, "Well, since you guys have rejected me as your king, I also reject you as my people. Now, I will dump you and choose another country that will acknowledge, accept, and take me as their king for life". No, God is not a man to change like that. He is not a politician. He is a great Leader and He demonstrated to mortals how leadership challenges should be handled. He is the Sovereign Ruler of the Ends of the earth who cannot be contested with or be voted out of power. He is God! He rules the earth including Israel of old and Nigeria.

Whether they acknowledge this or not does not change the fact and the truth that He is in charge. He knew His people had derailed and would someday run back to Him so He was waiting. But for the moment, He had to bear with them, and in the meantime, he kept His interest in them; He would not let them be destroyed by their enemies. He began to work backstage with His prophet Samuel to give them the king they asked for.

That is the same way He treats every other nation especially those that have acknowledged Him as God. The Holy Bible confirms this,

"Then Peter replied, 'I see very clearly that the Jews are not God's only favorites! In every nation he has those who worship him and do good deeds and are acceptable to him" (Acts 10 vs 34-35 TLB)

Although Israel disappointed God and His prophet, God went ahead and was involved in getting them the leader they requested. Our Book records:

"Now the LORD had told Samuel in the ear a day before Saul came, saying, To morrow about this time I will send thee a man out of the land of Benjamin, and thou shalt anoint him to be captain over my people Israel, that he may save my people out of the hand of the Philistines: for I have looked upon my people, because their cry is come unto me" (9 vs. 15-16)

God is a merciful and a compassionate Father. Yes, He is, but do not take Him for granted; He is also a consuming fire! Though "the people" had indirectly rejected Him, He still heard the cry of "the people". Note that it was the elders of the land that came together to Samuel requesting a national leader; a human government as it were. Not all the people of the land were involved in that conspiracy.

So I make bold to say that not the entire populace had agreed to that decision to bring in a human government. So the elders, that is, "the people" in the first instance that went to Samuel must have made that decision on behalf of themselves and the entire people in the name of national interest.

Therefore, because they considered themselves as the senior citizens with titles such as OON, OFR, MFR, MON, GCON, and GCFR, and because they were the distinguished senators and honorable members in the land, they held a national summit or national conference at Ramah, invited Samuel, the chief representative of Heaven's Parliament, and presented their alarming resolution: "We want a king!" They assumed the representation of the entire people of the land, and whatever they felt was right in their assumptions was right anyway.

They were certainly not among the people who cried unto the LORD as God told Samuel, because they had already taken their matter to Samuel, crying unto him, asking for a human king who would fight their battles. So while the people – possibly the masses who trusted in the saving arm of Jehovah cried unto Him for their deliverance, "the people", that is, the honorable members and senior citizens with multiple confusing titles cried unto Samuel for a leader to save them. Both camps needed deliverance but they went about it differently.

While the people who were considered the educated, enlightened elite class sought for a human captain, the people considered as illiterate and uneducated persons sought for a divine intervention – they cried unto the Captain of their salvation. Who then was wise? Anyway, God had to balance things. He heard the cry of the masses and the insult of the elites, but decided to give them a "deliverer". He told Samuel to anoint Saul of Benjamin to captain the people. That was how the people by themselves, through selfishness and ignorance, brought in military dictatorship in their country!

If we look carefully at and study the first few years of our country's independence, and how the military seized power, we might discover a similar case. When a people invite a wrong government, they should be prepared to get wrong governance. The military was never designed by God to bear rule over a nation, but to defend it against enemy invasion.

The first picture of an army that we see in the Holy Bible was in Abraham's time. It was when he raised an army of 318 trained servants and slaves of his to fight against four presidents: Amraphel of Shinar, Arioch of Ellasar, Chedorlaomer of Elam, and Tidal of Goiim (Genesis 14).

Abraham took his trained servants, armed them, and went to war to rescue his nephew. I guess that operation was tagged Operation Rescue Lot. It reminds me of 90 Minutes at Entebbe. Eventually, they rescued not only Lot but all others that were taken captive by those four presidents.

So the army or the military is to defend a nation and not to rule over them. That's the original plan of God. But our people invited the military to "stabilize" the nation, and indeed they stabilized it until they stabled our people like animals in their stable that made some of our people to begin to behave like humans with animal instincts. That was exactly what God told Samuel to warn his people of:

"If you insist on having a king, he will conscript your sons and make them run before his chariots...while others will be slave laborers; they will be forced to plow in the royal fields and harvest his crops without pay. He will demand your slaves and the finest of your youth and will use your animals for his personal gain" (8 vs. 11-12, 16 TLB)

Were these not what the junta did to our people in our countries and in our continent?

About three decades of military rule in Nigeria produced no lasting positive and creative development that we can boast of today. They were decades of chaotic developments cum abuse of executive jurisdiction that eventually birthed the ill-bred, lopsided, and illusory democracy that is being practiced in our land today, and thus circumvented the emergence of true federalism we needed. .

It was a time of gross abuse of human rights and the marginalization of progressive entities; where our good people worked and labored like monkeys without their correct wages. Indeed, it was a time when pensions were either denied or withheld for irrational reasons. A time when the conscience of men of honesty and integrity was mortgaged and the few that dared to speak out were either gagged or silenced forever.

If our people, I mean the so-called senior citizens had allowed the pain of the moment, and if they, of course, had cried to God instead of crying to the Khaki Boys, things would have been better for us all by now. It was an error they did not foresee was about to occur or maybe, they foresaw it but watched and even facilitated its occurrence for what they would gain then. Despite all, God remains true as God, and His plans and purposes will always stand.

So Saul, a goodly man he was though, emerged president and commander in chief on a platform of stubbornness, disobedience, disloyalty, and lack of confidence in God. He was a product of a warped system that swallowed up his goodliness and shaped him into compulsory consonance with the trends of that system. Hence, his government became characterized by the dictates of men rather than the doctrines of God.

...His Excellency

But before we go further to look at the errors of this unfortunate hero who ended woefully, we must note some good aspects of his life and leadership. This is our usual tradition in this series.

We refer to Saul as a hero in the first instance because God was aware and involved in his choice and election as the president and commander in chief of his country. Secondly, he was formally ordained and commissioned into that exalted office by God's chosen prophet, Samuel; he did not steal anybody's mandate neither did he plan a coup to oust any government before him.

As a matter of fact, the government before Saul's emergence was headed by God and ably represented by Prophet Samuel. So he did not overthrow Samuel nor did he overthrow God. In fact, Saul had no political ambition, and there is no record that he aspired for the leadership of his country. He was simply favored by the Council of Heaven to be captain over the people of his country.

Although God had registered His displeasure with the request by His chosen people for a human national leader, yet He never relinquished His ever-established position as their Supreme and Sovereign Leader – the Leader of every nation under heaven. We must note here that this earth is not under Satan. That is, the nations, tribes, tongues, and races of the Earth are not under the ruler ship of the Devil; God is in charge.

What Satan does is this: he hijacks the running of the system – the right to rule that God gave man, corrupts it, and gives it back to man to carry on with. And many on this earth who are not on God's side, therefore, operate the corrupt system. God rules the ends of the earth: this He even confirmed to Job and the Prophets of old. Whichever, God uses circumstances to work out the best for His people, and to promote His programs for His children in all the nations of the Earth.

But then, Saul's appearance on the stage was at a time when his country was yet to recover from the loss of the Ark of God which was captured by the enemies. It was a time when the giants of enemy nations assaulted the people of God and defied the name of Jehovah. It was a time when the enemies invaded their territory and took charge of economic and political affairs, and made the owners of the land prisoners and slaves. So Saul Kish had his hands full already from the first day of his resumption in office as the captain over God's people.

...The Setup

Now, to talk about the "goodliness" of Saul, we must begin from home. According to our history, his father Kish was a rich influential man – a man of power; a man of stalwart character. He had lost his donkeys – part of his merchandise, and then tasked Saul with the recovery. He had to take a servant along and look for the missing donkeys. And Saul did that. Now, that is obedience.

He did not begin to form a big-boy prince and say, "But Dad, why me? Why not send the chief servant of the house along with this servant to go get back the animals? I mean, Dad..." No, he did not do that; he simply followed his father's instructions. He was prepared and ready to run domestic errands for his father even when he knew the task of finding some lost animals whose location was uncertain was not that simple. Saul showed loyalty to his father by taking the pains to look for their lost business detail. History recorded that it took them a journey of about three days in search of the lost donkeys till they ran into the prophet of God, Samuel.

To further show the goodliness of Saul, he humbled himself to listen to his servant at the time he wanted to call off the search when they could not find the missing donkeys. History informs us:

"When they got to Zuph, Saul said to the young man with him, 'Enough of this. Let us go back. Soon my father is going to forget about the donkeys and start worrying about us!' He replied, 'Not so fast. There's a holy man in this town. He carries a lot of weight around here. What he says is always right on the mark. Maybe he can tell us where to go'... 'Good,' said Saul, 'let us go.' And they set off for the town where the holy man lived" (9 vs 5-8, 10 TM)

The scripture above was a dialogue between Saul and the servant with him on the search mission. The search had come to a dead end – no luck! Saul had decided it was time to quit and go home, but his servant objected, and then suggested they visit Prophet Samuel in the town for help. Saul humbled himself and listened to the advice and persuasion of a mere servant.

When they finally reached the prophet's place and were well received, he and his servant were meek to follow all of the holy man's instructions and directions. This quality showed that history's record of Saul's goodliness beside his handsomeness was true and affirmative. Finally the anointing of God came upon his life. Our Book then says,

"Do you see what this means? God has anointed you prince over his people...Before you know it, the Spirit of God will come on you and you'll be prophesying right along...And you'll be transformed. You'll be a new person!" (10 vs. 1, 6 TM)

Saul Kish became a new man, but not for long, I guess. How does this concern us?

Our own leaders came up singing different songs of transformation: how they would transform our dear country, and all that. But I thought they should have told us how transformed they were themselves; their encounters with God's transformation Agent – the Holy Spirit, or at least, shown us the evidence of their personal transformation. This is because it only takes a man who is truly transformed to sing a song of transformation and to effect transformation policies in the nation.

I believe that the greatest transformation song there can be is that of the man or woman who wants to be an agent of transformation. It is not enough to gather some popular songwriters to put together a good song on transformation for you to perform in order to woo us; do best to woo us by the story of your personal transformation encounter. And we must also know who you had the encounter with – God or the no-gods.

However, an encounter with God does not even guarantee that such a man is transformed because some people do not allow God to complete the divine due process of transformation in their lives before they hit the campaign grounds announcing their encounter and the agenda they have for the people. That is why all the transformation agendas of our heroes never yielded lasting positive results. This is because they were not thoroughly baked in God's oven of transformation, so they could not produce transformation.

They may allow the process to go on right in the presence of the prophet but once they receive what they want, the process is aborted. It all ends a mirage. That's why the new personality of Saul did not last till the end of his life even though he had demonstrated that he was a new man.

...The Presentation

So after that demonstration at Gibeah, his hometown, and his people's astonishment at his new personality, the official presentation took place at Mizpah. It was the presentation of the preferred candidate to fly the flag of the People's Disobedience to God Party, PDGP. No other party was acknowledged.

The opposition was not strong and capable enough to field someone, so Saul was the only candidate. Or maybe, God did not permit the opposition to summon the needed courage to produce their man since He was involved in the whole "setup". Saul's father and other PDGP chieftains had probably rallied other towns to get support from tribal heads, and maybe had promised them or their children compensations with ministerial or other appointments. Politics, it is.

Every program of God presents us with the temptation of running our own things, and the opportunity of allowing God to run things through us – two different things. But unfortunately, many despise the opportunity because it does not put them directly in charge and they would not take the glory for running things. Thus, they fall into the temptation and are destroyed in the end. So, His Excellency was presented to the people, and the prophet remarked,

"Take a good look at whom God has chosen: the best! No one like him in the whole country! Then a great shout went up: 'Long live the king! (10 vs. 24 TM)

...The Peoples' Response

It was a welcome development in the land! However, with all the "goodliness" of our hero, some people, probably part of the opposition, who the Bible described as riffraff, bums and loafers, children of Belial, went off muttering, ***"Deliverer? Do not make me*** *laugh!"* (vs. 27 TM) They said among themselves, ***"How can this man save us?"***

And the Holy Bible recorded that Saul, the president-elect, took no notice, and paid them no mind. Maybe he was still overwhelmed by the fact that though he came ***"from the smallest of Israel's tribes, and from the most insignificant clan in the tribe at that"*** he was chosen by God as his country's leader.

Though he had no political ambition to lead his country, yet he found himself faced with the reality of heading a national government – the first ever in the history of his country after the era of the Judges. It was a task of which he had no other choice than to accept. It was the "will" of God for him because God was involved in his election. And since it was the ordinance of the Most High God, there was nothing anybody could do about it. They just had to welcome it.

Can you think of any of our national leaders whose emergence at the scene of national leadership of our country could be likened to that of Saul? Was there (or is there) any president or head of state and commander in chief you can recall whose candidacy could be likened to that of Saul? Well, let me leave you to answer that. In any case, the end of a man, President Solomon David said, is better than his beginning. With all this talk about the choice of this hero being the "will" of God though in response to the request of the people, he still failed.

Now, we can confidently deduce and conclude from our reliable Bible records that the straying donkeys and Saul's search mission to recover them were all orchestrated by God in order to lead him to the holy man at Ramah. Remember that history revealed that

"The very day before, God had confided in Samuel, 'This time tomorrow, I am sending a man from the land of Benjamin to meet you. You're to anoint him as prince over my people Israel. He will free my people from Philistine oppression. Yes, I know all about their hard circumstances. I've heard their cries for help" (9 vs. 15-16 TM)

Emphatically, Saul's emergence as president was not an accident; God made it so. Then, why did he fail God?

<u>...Prepared For the Task?</u>

Now, I hate to ask this question over and over, but we cannot help but ask it. Why did he fail? He had only one mandate; one agenda: to free his country from Philistine oppression but he died in a battle against the Philistines unaccomplished! His country still remained under the oppression of the Philistines! Was he not prepared for the mandate? I do not think so.

Samuel had told him by the inspiration and Spirit of God the things that would happen to confirm that he was the chosen one.

"When these confirming signs are accomplished, you'll know that you're ready: Whatever job you're given to do, do it. God is with you!" (10 vs. 7 TM)

That is it! What else did he need? He was given a sign that would show to him that he was ready and prepared for the leadership job, and that whatever assignment God would entrust to his care, he should not fail to do it. And indeed, all those signs came to pass before he got home, even before his official presentation and swearing-in.

He was filled with the Spirit of God and he prophesied alongside a band of well-known prophets. He was ordained and sworn-in in the presence of all his country men and women, and they hailed him as Mr. President. He did not object to his election neither did he reject his ordination as His Excellency; he welcomed it in humility and with a ready heart to serve his fatherland. Yet, years later, he failed as Mr. President.

The fact that His Excellency understood the assignment God gave him – the task ahead of him – cannot be overemphasized. He was to deliver and free his people from the all-powerful enemy occupying their territory. As a General, he knew what was required of him. He did not need any other person to explain further the portfolio of a head of state and commander in chief. If he however needed further tutoring, Samuel had just done that at his election, induction, and coronation ceremonies. Yet he failed.

Saul, as a young man after he was chosen, was not a foolish man. He was a wise young man. He displayed great wisdom and intelligence when he returned from the ordination ground at Samuel's place.

His uncle who also could be a powerful man in the society had been worried that Saul his nephew was not back from the search for the straying donkeys. He must have joined his brother Saul's father in praying for his safe return since the donkeys had found their way back to the stable – God's design. The animals simply obeyed the nudging of God's Spirit and left their master's stable in order to connect Saul to Samuel – destiny. And after their mission was accomplished, the Spirit of God moved them to go back home without the search team setting their eyes on them. Then the search team of Saul and his servant had not returned home after three days.

As the whole Kish family waited for the safe return of their noble son with the attendant worry and anxiety and apprehension, suddenly there was news that Saul had been found prophesying along with well-known prophets at Gibeah. The news filtered into his family's compound and into the ears of his waiting uncle.

You know how some uncles behave: they want to know the details. They often want to know why it is their nephews that experience such things and not their own sons. He must have reasoned that nothing of such – Saul prophesying – could have happened on its own without an encounter with a holy man. So then, the Bible records,

"And Saul's uncle said unto him and unto his servant, Whither went ye? And he said, To seek the asses: and when we saw that they were nowhere, we came to Samuel. And Saul's uncle said, Tell me, I pray thee, what Samuel said unto you: And Saul said unto his uncle, He told us plainly that the asses were found. But of the matter of the kingdom, whereof Samuel spake, he told him not" (10 vs. 13-16)

So Saul was not foolish to discuss the matter of the kingdom of Israel with his uncle. He was wise to restrain himself. In other words, he demonstrated self-control and kept the matter to himself. *"Tell me, I pray thee"* implied that his uncle practically persuaded him to narrate the details of his encounter with Samuel the holy man to him. But Saul, by the Spirit of God, did not open up. Bible record says, *"But he did not tell him that he had been anointed as king"* (TLB). Is that not wisdom?

Some young men of our day and even those of his day could brag about it. They might begin to boast to their uncle about their dining and wining with the highest prophet in the land. Some would have carelessly sold out their destiny to people who God saw but bypassed to choose them.

For the youth who lacks discernment and prudence, they would start parading town announcing their encounter with the holy man, and even go declaring their nomination and endorsement as the president-elect. After all, there was no other human king in his country at that time to challenge him, and if anyone had bothered him, he would have quickly referred them to Prophet Samuel. But Saul Kish did not do so. Instead, he maintained his cool and humble disposition, gave his uncle just a chapter of his encounter with the prophet, and kept the most exciting and most important unpublished pages to his chest. Our Book stressed that *"the matter of the kingdom whereof Samuel spake"*, he told his uncle nothing. Great display of wisdom! Yet Saul failed.

We may not be able in this book to give full details of Saul's good side; the Bible is there for all to study for themselves. The much we have seen suggest that Saul was, slightly above average, a good man. But why did he then fail? Why do some good people fail to live up to expectation even when they're chosen and ordained by God?

...The Institution

To answer these questions, we must go back to what God told Samuel to tell the people of his country when they made that foolish request. He said,

"But warn them of what they're in for. Tell them the way kings (human governments) ***operate, just what they're likely to get from a king*** (human leader)***"*** Emphasis added.

So, it is a matter of the institution – the platform rather than the personality. The Council of Heaven or Heaven's Parliament was actually pointing to them the system: not necessarily the personality of President Saul, but the "personality" which the system would compel him to become as soon as he assumes office.

Remember that the system and the umbrella that requested a human government were already on ground before the emergence of Saul. As a matter of fact, he was not a part of that system that felt God their Supreme Leader and His government was inadequate and so they needed a seemingly impacting leader – a necessity God permissively granted.

And to say that Saul was a bad man before he even ascended the throne would be to assert that God enthrones bad kings and corrupt leaders to rule His people. This is not true.

To say that Saul was actually going to be a bad example of leadership would be to imply a contradiction of God's Word and to insinuate that God's assignment to Saul was a pseudo-act and just a cover-up since there's a foreknowledge of his potential failure as a national leader. It would also translate into saying that the ordinance of God with regards to leadership especially the leadership of a country chosen by God is error-prone. God forbid!

Jehovah does not make mistakes. Whatever He declares is true, and He has no hidden agenda for the world. This is because He is God and no one can call Him to account for anything; He is not answerable to anyone even though He is so humble to reason with His creation. The reason why God declares for Saul was for the assignment He gave him: To deliver His people from Philistine oppression. No more, no less.

However, God knows that man is not stable in character. He knew that those who had requested a human king and had rejected Him could manipulate the human king to their own presumed advantage. And that would certainly jeopardize the entire program He has for the people. That is why He gave the warning.

So many people who find themselves as elder statesmen have become manipulators of the leadership of their nations because they believe that they are the wise ones. And any governor or president who is not wary of them might fall for them.

Now having satisfied to an extent the question of our hero's understanding of his portfolio as head of state; that he really understood the mandate and was ready for it, why then did he fail? Why did he not fulfil the mandate? Why did he begin in the spirit but ended in the flesh? At least he was once filled with the Spirit of God and he prophesied so then why did he end up a disappointment?

Why would a man who dined and wined with a holy man – the number one holy man of his day, and received the mantle of leadership on a platter fail? Why would a goodly man perform badly even with the strong backing of divinity and the heavy presence of the anointing? Simple: he took all for granted and allowed an error into his life.

CHAPTER TWO

WHAT HAVE YOU DONE?

...Reflections

It has been well established so far that President Saul was obedient to his biological father and also to Prophet Samuel in doing all they told him to do. It is also true that he listened to the voice of his search-team-mate – the servant that later went to Ramah with him. Then, why could not he listen and obey the voice of the same Samuel after he had become president and commander in chief? Why did His Excellency disobey the same voice he had obeyed years before he became the leader of his country?

Samuel, God's ambassador to Israel had addressed the people of his country thus:

"Behold, I have hearkened unto your voice in all that ye said unto me, and have made a king over you. Now therefore, behold the king whom ye have chosen, and whom ye have desired, and behold, the LORD hath set a king over you. If ye will fear the LORD, and serve him, and obey his voice, and not rebel against the commandment of the LORD, then shall both ye and also the king that reigneth over you continue following the LORD your God: But if ye will not obey the voice of the LORD...then shall the hand of the LORD be against

you...ye shall be consumed, both ye and your king"
(12 vs. 1, 13-15, 25)

This was a national charge delivered by Heaven's ambassador, Samuel.

After the first conquest of Saul over the Ammonites, the people had confirmed his election and presidency. Amidst the excitement and nationwide jubilation that their dream of a national hero had begun to come to pass, Samuel took them to Gilgal – a place of renewal of oath and re-dedication of the government – and presented them to God. There also the kingdom of Israel and the kingship of Saul were dedicated to God.

It was the beginning of the harvest of the dividends of the new government, probably democracy. Dashed dreams and quashed hopes and aspirations began to resurrect. Life was beginning to become worth living once again.

The news of the conquest of the nation of Ammon circulated through the press across the entire country and beyond. The enslaved people were beginning to get their freedom from their enemies and slave masters. And our Book recorded that **"Saul and all the men of Israel rejoiced greatly"** (11:5). Maybe he had declared a public holiday to celebrate his conquest and everyone stayed at home to celebrate that deserved victory. Maybe too, his political party, the PDGP had seized the moment and had organized press conferences to further position their "dear" party for consolidation but under the guise of affirming their government's commitment to the welfare of the state, and their readiness to give total liberation to the people.

They may have also dedicated that victory to the Ambassador, Prophet Samuel for listening to their voice and had given them their hearts' desire. Or maybe they had declared that it was victory for their nascent "democracy". They may have also called on all the people of the land to give their man, President Saul, their unalloyed support to be able to deliver more dividends promptly.

I can picture the main opposition – those **"children of Belial"** – holding meetings and praying that the new president should make a costly mistake that would present them with the opportunity to discredit the ruling party. They may also have held their peace during the time of the nationwide feasting since it was conspicuously clear that the people welcomed that conquest of Ammon as a long-awaited, long-expected, and overdue positive development. There was nothing the opposition could do about it at that material time. If they kicked against the declaration of the public holiday by the ruling party, the entire people would, doubtless, have regarded them as enemies of national progress.

If they had gone to the tribunal to challenge the emergence of His Excellency as president as some people in our land would do, this clear victory would have shut them up. If not, the chieftains and stalwarts of the ruling party would be compelled to use some tutored thugs to shut them up.

I want to clearly state that although the Bible described this opposition group as "children of Belial" yet not all opposition parties are children of Belial. It was obvious that this opposition party in the days of President Saul and his People's Disobedience to God Party was not recognized and backed up by Heaven's Parliament.

However, in Bible times, God did raise oppositions against some leaders who failed the true test of leadership and betrayed their divine mandates. Even in our days, God still raises and stirs up opposition against defaulting leaders in governments, corporate organizations, and even in religious houses. A stubborn member of a Church council may be there to check the priest's excesses. I have seen that, you know.

So Saul became the people's hero since the opposition could do nothing. His petty heroism was on all newspaper headlines, that is, if they had a functional press at that time. I believe they had them. "President

Saul Humbles Nahash of Ammon" could be the leading headline on all national dailies, or any other caption that would sell the papers – the editors' magic!

You remember the big story: **"Obama Kills Osama"** and the world stood in awe and ovation of the African-American US president. It was like that in the time of Saul. But in the midst of the celebration of the fall of President Nahash and his country, Heaven saw the most urgent need of the hour: Renewal and Re-dedication at Gilgal! Then, they sent their Ambassador, Samuel.

This was what our country's past heroes did not see. They were so blinded by their ungodly quest for the rulership of the country and of the continent that they forgot the weightier matters of an independent state. Like I noted earlier at the beginning of this chapter, our first generation national heroes resorted to force – a necessary evil – because they lacked the understanding of how to make things work in a newly independent state.

So when they could no longer endure the excesses of the military that they had invited to stabilize the nation, they began to groan and moan under the taskmanship of the junta, and consequently called for the quittance of the unholy military rule. But their call was ignored for a long time.

The holy man had set out a time for the rituals for renewal and re-dedication, but His Excellency set out to fight the hard-fighting, never-say-die Philistines. Victory, you know, is sweet and even sweeter when the hero is widely applauded and celebrated, and also when it is specially dedicated to the people for their overwhelming support. Our history Book records,

"And it was so on the morrow, that...they came into the midst of the host in the morning watch, and slew the Ammonites until the heat of the day...And the people said unto Samuel, Who is he that said, Shall Saul reign over us? Bring the men, that we may put them to death. And Saul said, There shall not a man be put to death this day: for today the LORD hath wrought salvation in Israel" (11 vs. 11-13)

Another character display!

The people, probably some heavy weights in his political party had proposed the prosecution and execution of the opposition members for not publicly acknowledging and accepting His Excellency as the new president. But Mr. President threw out the proposal and said, *"Nobody is going to be executed this day. This is the day God saved Israel"* (TM).

Here, President Saul again demonstrated tolerance – one lesson for our contemporary leaders. They have got to learn how to tolerate the opposition. But our dear heroes had fallen short of this very vital virtue.

Our leaders at all levels and various capacities should learn and imbibe the spirit of tolerance and compromise in the interest of peace especially when it is obvious that God is in control of events and circumstances. After all, the opposition only expressed their feeling about the administration of Mr. President setting things right in their country; they did not incite anybody against him nor did they cause any deaths.

Another lesson our contemporary Nigerian and African leaders must learn and uphold is embedded in the next biblical record: ***"He (Saul) put the people in three companies"***. This means that he recognized the fact that a leader needs to carry the people along in the leadership of the nation. The people wanted a king that would go before them, and they got one that actually recognized their importance. This is called the people-factor. However, in winning the love of the people, this important ingredient should not come before the God-factor. Moreover, the people that must be carried along must not be forced to go along; they must be willing to go along!

President Saul realized that for the country's nascent democracy or whatever to be strengthened; for the war against oppression to be won, the people –

politicians and masses, elites and commons, learned and unlearned – must be integrated into the governance of the country. And so when the war against President Nahash of Ammon was won, President Saul probably dedicated the victory to the people for their undivided hearts and unflagging support. The entire populace loved it and fell so much in love with him. To them, the victory came at the right time.

And because His Excellency celebrated the people for their patriotism, they encouraged him to go ahead and engage the dreaded Philistines in a fierce battle to end their oppression. It was one war they had expected; the battle the elders and the senior citizens had looked forward to. It was this expectation that moved them to request for a champion that would go before them in battle – the battle against the monsters called Philistines. But it was a battle that needed the God-factor to be successful.

...Waiting at Gilgal

A flashback to history reminded them of several assaults that those uncircumcised breed had carried out on their country. Then, they had no anointed head of state but judges, priests, and prophets. Now that they have got a military man of valor as their commander in chief, nothing was going to stop them from getting total deliverance from those enemies.

If I were there, I would not blame them. This is because every nation seeks a man who would take responsibility and lead them to total victory over numerous monstrous challenges facing them as a nation. Nevertheless, such challenges are not to be rushed into without adequate preparation. Ill preparation, oftentimes, is the bane of failure.

No matter how skilled a leader is, it is advisable to take into full cognizance the nature of the challenges facing his community, constituency, or country before launching a solution campaign. This is one area most of our past heroes failed. That was why Prophet Samuel instructed, by the word of God, that His Excellency and his government should hold on for seven days before launching the offensive. That's right. Seven days of purification; seven days of getting instructions and directions from God before the final and compulsory ritual at Gilgal. Although Jerusalem was the seat of government, Gilgal had become the place of consecration, coronation, and consolidation of His Excellency and his administration in his days.

While Aso Rock remains the place of executing our country's affairs, the Rock of Ages remains the Only Place of consecration and consolidation for any leader who must win the battles facing his government in order to record success. Hence, there must be a waiting there! Seven days had to be observed for total victory to be assured.

The number "seven", theologians say, biblically connotes perfection. His Excellency was instructed to wait on God for the perfect day so that his agenda and mandate of delivering his people from Philistine oppression would not fail. But what was he going to wait there for all the time?

For us, it could be a period of self-examination – for the leaders and their subordinates; kings and their subjects; governments and their cabinets; a time of examination and cross examination, and a complete assessment that would build our faith in God, boost our resolve to launch the offensive, and produce the determination and will to fight to finish all forms of challenges facing our independent states. It is indeed a time to decide to lynch and eradicate corruption from the system in order to pilot the affairs of the state successfully. But our heroes, like Saul, failed.

Down memory lane in our dear land, our military and civilian leaders in their various dispensations had come face to face with great challenges of leading our people to total freedom out of the quagmire of the hard-life which was a result of the several irregularities and bad governance by preceding administrations.

There had been times in their era when the need to pull out the suffering neglected people of our country from the pit of hellish frustration and lack became intensely urgent. They had experienced the pressure of modifying existing policies and even bilateral relations with other entities in order to remedy the so-messed up circumstances and give the country a face-lift.

Our heroes no doubt must have experienced times in their dispensations, in their different positional capacities when the amendment of some sections of already existing laws appeared the only way out of the nation's political nightmare and economic instability.

Not leaving out our spiritual leaders who at one time or the other might have come to the point where they had to decide either in favor of time-tested godly doctrines as endorsed by God or in favor of dogmatic realities that contrast those doctrines but support their inconsistent bigotry.

In fact, the catalogue of our leaders' experiences similar to the few listed above is endless. Yet, they were times to wait on the Almighty God for instructions, guidance, and direction. They were times to patiently look up to God who knows the best strategies and approaches that definitely guarantee solutions and success.

For the politicians, it was time to listen attentively to the voice of God through His anointed prophets. For the anointed prophets, it was time to listen to the Holy Spirit speaking expressly to them and through other prophets.

But what did our heroes do? Did they wait? No. Did they listen to the voice of God? No. Did they listen to His prophets? No! Just like Saul who, in a bid to sustain the victory trend, keep the winning ways and pace, and keep the flag of their party flying high above all others, foolishly engaged the hard-fighting Philistines in that war.

"Philistine oppression" could mean economic sabotage, political savages, social vices, high-level spiritual harlotry, psychological torture and torment caused by poverty, and total deviation from all godly pursuits. Philistine oppression contrasts all forms of godliness but condones all forms of wickedness. That is why the people of God must be free from their grip. **But "not by power, not by might, but by my Spirit, saith the LORD"**. Prophet Jeremiah cried out,

"I know, God, that mere mortals can not run their own lives, that men and women do not have what it takes to take charge of life" (10 vs. 23 TM)

That is the truth; nothing far from it. It does not mean that man cannot handle life at all; it means that man can only handle and survive life by hanging on God. This is the God-factor. If the God-factor had been thoroughly and carefully considered and embraced, the war against those monsters would have been totally won.

<u>...First Things First</u>

The Book of First Samuel chapter thirteen opens up with a brief on Mr. President who had ruled for about two years or more over his country. What he was doing the whole time were not all written in our history pages. But the available, reliable information revealed that he was busy recruiting and training men for the final showdown against the Philistines. His Excellency was preoccupied with winning the war that he forgot the weightier matter – the preparation for the final ritual of re-dedication that the nation's prophet had fixed.

Our Excellences forgot the mandatory retreat and the time of sober reflection before The Most Excellent King, Jehovah, and they got busy with their own insignificant mandates and agenda. The whole time, they were busy with fitness test for the men who would go down hard on the dreaded opposition or corruption as the case may be. They did not create time for God.

They did not have time to study the Law of God and to meditate on it in order for them to have good success. They did not bother to offer personal sacrifices to God in order to know His mind on the proposed war against injustice, oppression, poverty, idolatry, or corruption. They did not even study history very well to know what made preceding administrations to fail, and how they could get a clue from their experiences to succeed. They just believed that they had the joker to win the game since they regard politics as a game.

While War against Indiscipline (WAI), Operation Feed the Nation, Kick Against Indiscipline (KAI), Mass Mobilization for Self-Reliance, Social Justice and Economic Recovery (MAMSER), and the Rebranding Nigeria Campaign were all good programs, the need to table them before the Council of Heaven was more important than the pursuit for their realization. There was hardly any battle that President David Jesse fought that he did not first make inquiry from God. And that is why he did not lose any one.

During America's worst economic recession of the 1930s, some of their leaders had reminded their counterparts and the entire people of their lands how their founding fathers fought to secure their independence and to sustain it. It was the God-factor they inculcated into their thoughts and incorporated into their plans and programs that gave them the victory over those nagging years.

In an European newspaper of June 10, 1993, former USSR leader Mikhail Gorbachev stated in a state of the world address that **"It is obvious that our civilization is reaching the end of the line...The crisis reflects most graphically the crisis of the Spirit...What is needed today...is an atmosphere of spirituality. Let us recall the prophetic words of St. Paul: 'You must change by renewing your minds.'"** Gorbachev was right. The first step in preparing for victory over all of man's troubles is the renewing of the mind.

First things first: The US founding fathers knew that and so anchored their faith and philosophy on God, and they had victory. Inscribed on their currency is IN GOD WE TRUST, and that's why they are leading the rest of the world!

What, if I may ask, did our own founding fathers do? What did they inscribe on our own currency? Where did they put their trust? In God or in themselves? It is not enough to sing: "O God of Creation, Direct Our Noble Cause..." in the National Anthem; making those words a part of our legislative, judicial, and executive affairs should be the in-thing. First things first! EFCC, ICPC, Oputa Panel, KAI, WAI, etc. - failed and are failing because they were not established on the premise of true democratic values and right motives.

President Saul thought that recruiting men for war against oppression was the secret to winning it, but he was dead wrong. History tells us that

"Saul conscripted enough men for three companies of soldiers. He kept two companies under his command at Michmash and in the Bethel hills. The other company was under Jonathan at Gibeah in Benjamin" (13 vs. 2 TM)

...Negligence of the God-Factor

Let us not digress into the significance of those locations of his three companies so that we can really look at a more important issue – his errors.

What happened next? Good news! Jonathan killed the Philistine governor at Geba, that is, Gibeah, their own home zone. The news spread so fast. At least, part of the mission is accomplished. The local press did not waste time to publish it on front pages and as headline news. Meanwhile, the international communities were alarmed because they knew what it was like killing a Philistine governor or an ambassador by the revolting, freedom-thirsty Jews. The Bible further says,

"Saul has killed the Philistine governor – drawn first blood! The Philistines are stirred up and mad as hornets!" (13 vs. 4 TM)

The momentary takeover of Gibeah from the enemies stirred them up to fight back to reclaim that town; it did not dampen their spirit.

If you remember vividly the recent uprisings in some countries north of Africa, you would recall that some towns were captured by rebels and the government forces did not go to sleep. There were several capturing and recapturing, claiming and reclaiming of major towns and cities during those difficult times until one camp finally took over. That was the picture. What were they fighting for? Simple: the control of the states and their resources – who rules.

Most times, ill preparation before embarking on a project or before executing an agenda of great magnitude often leads to the awakening of unseen potential and unpredictable challenges. To hurry into a national mandate or assignment with presumed knowledge of how to achieve it without adequate preparation and without the incorporation of the God-factor will ultimately lead to absolute chaos, waste of resources, and a harvest of avoidable regrets. Making such moves without consulting well with Heaven's Parliament and getting their backing will doubtless result to a nightmare or a daydream!

President David Jesse often boasted of the victories that heaven gave him over his challenges, and it was primarily because he consulted with God: the reason God called him "a man after my own heart".

But for our past heroes, they failed. It can also happen to the present crop of emerging heroes if they fail like Saul, and also if they fail to learn the brazen lessons so far highlighted in this series. My constant prayer for all who read this timely piece of divine inspiration is that they do not allow the errors of our heroes of old to repeat in their own lives.

Prophet Samuel had set a time for the sacrifice that would attract the mercy of God, appease Heaven's Parliament, and guarantee total backing for the establishment of the reign of His Excellency: putting to eternal halt the oppression of the Philistines and other enemy nations. But there was a problem, an error which had rooted itself in the system. It was an error that all the strategies mapped out by Saul's administration could not correct. It had to do with the foundation of the platform on which he emerged as Mr. President. It was a problem that even his special advisers could not nip in the bud nor proffer solution to because it was a result of the crack in the foundation of that system.

The error can be deduced from the following scriptures which contain the message of God through Samuel to the people at the convocation at Mizpah.

"This is God's personal message to you: "I brought Israel up out of Egypt. I delivered you from Egyptian

oppression – yes, from all the bullying governments that made your life miserable. And now you want nothing to do with your God, the very God who has a history of getting you out of troubles of all sorts. And now you say, 'No, we want a king; give us a king!' Well, if that's what you want, that's what you'll get" (10 vs 18-19 TM)

Getting the idea? It was the same with our past heroes. The system which they pioneered and managed created lots of problems for successive administrations for which they could not find ways to solve. Maybe they could not solve those problems because the problems would have taken some ego-crushing, pride-smashing experience to solve. And since they were not ready to make that sacrifice, they decided to leave the stage of national service messed up. They left that as legacy for us.

President Saul thought that two years of recruiting and training an army was a very good strategy in ending the Philistine oppression. He forgot that new levels would automatically introduce and attract new devils; that the opposition would raise their level of resistance once there is an attack on them. He did not however realize that a large cabinet of confused party loyalists whom he selected to make compensations for their support during the election was no solution to the enormous challenges facing his administration and his country.

Some of our leaders, once they assume office would begin to consider their political party faithful, who in one way or another supported them during elections, for one office or the other. Whether those party faithful are really faithful or not is not their business as long as they belong to their political party.

Men who should naturally go back to their shops, garages, warehouses and factories to continue with their normal business of buying and selling, manufacturing and production, transportation and distribution of goods, find themselves at the presidential villa, office of the governor, or any government agency for allocation of various portfolios. Some of them who are not scholastically, precisely or proficiently qualified for such lofty offices and are therefore not considered for any, get massive contracts to do what they are virgins at.

Men who never humbled themselves by submitting to the norms of a godly society and by serving their communities well; whose major preoccupation all their vain lives has been the business of making money from the society without a commensurate impact on the environment. Men whose bellies are their gods and they invest heavily on frivolities, and therefore have developed pot-bellies – their only physical testimonials; liabilities to themselves and to the nation.

These are men who any responsible government should keep at bay to continue with their buying and selling, etc., while the business of governance is left to those divinely called to do it without distraction. But His Excellency did not do what any responsible leader is expected to do. Instead, he, I strongly believe, packed his cabinet full with wisdom-deficient PDGP loyalists who introduced to him the other side of leadership called politics. Then, what was the result? Our history says,

"When the Israelites saw that they were way outnumbered and in deep trouble, they ran for cover, hiding in caves and pits, ravines and brambles and cisterns – wherever. They retreated across the Jordan River, refugees fleeing to the country of Gad and Gilead. But Saul held his ground in Gilgal, his soldiers still with him but scared to death" (13 vs. 6-7 TM)

Imagine that. What a shame! That is the disadvantage of misplacement of priority – putting self before and ahead of God, and setting an agenda without the backing of Heaven's Parliament. The army that took His Excellency about two years to put together became scared to death!

The men who the president, governor, senator, director, bishop, vice chancellor, his royal majesty, etc., relied on to end the age-long siege and woeful assaults on their domain became afraid of engaging the challenges. Cowards! Wasted years of training! Wasted resources! Efforts in futility! Who then gained? Of course the international communities including the opposition they went out to face, I mean, the Philistines. The bible revealed that:

"There wasn't a blacksmith to be found anywhere in Israel. The Philistines made sure of that – 'Lest those Hebrews start making swords and spears.' That meant that the Israelites had to go down among the Philistines to keep their farm tool...sharp and in good repair...So when the battle of Michmash was joined, there wasn't a sword or spear to be found anywhere in Israel – except for Saul and his son Jonathan; they were well armed" (13 vs. 19-22 TM)

Do you see the problem? This is what I am talking about – ill preparation!

How could His Excellency recruit and train an army for two years without first making plans on how to equip them? In our country we hear of one agenda or the other by the president, the governor, the house of assembly, the director-general, the party leader, the chairman, or the chief executive.

But ask them what machineries or modalities they have put in place to actualize their agenda, you might be shocked to find out they have none. Or you might hear that plans are on the way, or still, the machineries are in the pipeline. Maybe that is why our pipelines are being vandalized from time to time by those who perhaps do not want the machineries to surface. And most times, they never surface!

It is not enough to declare your X or Y-point agenda; the devil is not scared of that. In fact, challenges and oppositions are not moved by that. They will only be moved when they see your strong moves in the right direction backed by Heaven. The reason is quite simple: oppositions know how to frustrate your agenda by going ahead of you with their own agenda and plans. President Saul could not arm his army well because the monsters he was trying to battle had made sure of that.

Have you ever wondered why several projects launched by our leaders never yielded success? It's because the opposition to the realization of those projects and programs had made sure they did not work. These oppositions may not necessarily be human beings, they can be existing anti-progress structures, bilateral relations, bureaucracies, and policies birthed by the past heroes.

Some of our past leaders who believed in the doctrine of social inequality or inequality of other sorts during their time established some policies and structures that successive administrations found no small matter trying to dismantle. This is why it is very important to set priorities right, lay the foundations solid on the right values; get it right from the start before announcing the agenda. This is also because once the agenda is announced; "oppositions" would equally announce their plans to frustrate your agenda when you set out to actualize them.

But for His Excellency, he announced the War against Philistine Oppression (WAPO) without first addressing the serious issue of arms and ammunition that his army would use which of course, his enemies made sure were out of his reach. The enemies knew that once Saul had mounted the throne, he would lead his country to revolt against them. From the time the elders and senior citizens called for a national conference at Ramah with the nation's prophet Samuel in attendance, the enemies began monitoring the political situations and the movements of those elites. They became aware that their lordship over the Hebrews would soon be challenged, and that could mean they might declare war. Finally, their suspicion was confirmed by the choice of Saul Kish of Benjamin, the tallest man in the whole land!

Even though Saul was from the least important family of the smallest tribe of Israel, yet the enemies knew the history of the character of his tribe. When their founder

Jacob was foretelling his children their future, he made mention of what to expect from Benjamin:

"Benjamin shall ravin as a wolf: in the morning he shall devour the prey, and at night he shall divide the spoil" (Genesis 49 vs. 27)

That was all he said about Benjamin where Saul descended from. History also confirmed this character of the Benjamites, and the Philistine lords knew this. So they were well prepared when the candidature of Saul was announced, and they began ahead of the Hebrews to put in place compulsory measures to nip in the bud any form of revolt.

So many of our heroes claim to be well versed in history but they have severally failed to learn from their predecessors. Now God wants them to learn from the Philistines and that is why He asked me to write it down for them, that is, if only they would learn.

Now, what was missing in Saul's camp? Simple: The God-factor! God's presence was missing. And you ask, how? His Excellency and his government by the ruling party did not learn from history. They did not learn from Moses the first national leader of their country who, with the pillar of cloud by day and the pillar of fire by night – symbols of God's presence – delivered their nation from the all-powerful Egyptians. They did not also learn from Gideon who, with only three hundred mere men defeated the Midianites and freed his country from their oppression.

One with God, they say, is majority. The secret of Gideon's victory and his successful defeat of the major challenge of his country is contained in the greeting of the Angel of God: ***"The LORD is with thee, thou mighty man of valor"*** (Judges 6:12). He was a mighty man of valor but he was running away and hiding from the challenges facing his country because he did not know that God was with him. Read the scriptures, man. He had the potential but he did not have the knowledge of the God-factor. That is why he replied the Angel:

"Oh my Lord, if the LORD be with us, why then is all this befallen us? And where be all his miracles which our fathers told us of, saying, Did not the LORD bring us up from Egypt?" (vs.13)

You see, he knew history but did not study well to learn the vital things from history. God is not a magician; He is a miracle working God! What He did for the people of old, He is ready to do even for us. But we must take the responsibility of activating God's presence to work for us. That was why Samuel told His Excellency to wait at Gilgal for seven days.

The Lord is with us, but are we with the Lord? The Lord wants to perform wonders, but are we prepared to wait on Him to do so? How many of our past leaders, I mean the ones that are still alive, can boldly and truthfully say that in their time, they were with God? How many of the present breed can even declare that indeed, they are with God?

Some might say, "Yes, we are with God; we are on God's side," but in reality, God has in His record that they have been on their own. Because you cannot be with God and remain the same; there must be a transformation. The problem is not God being with us; He is always there for us. But some of us have abandoned Him long ago even though they still claim that all is well. Because if you say that you are with God and He is with you, well, how come corruption which is one of devil's inventions still parades our land, wreaking havoc on our economy? Why have we been reeling to and fro in darkness, depression, and destitution?

Get this straight: All is well does not mean God is there, and this is for those who would say that, at least, they have been enjoying relative peace. God may be with you but the acknowledgement of His presence and giving Him space in your life is what makes His presence count.

For President Saul, all the while there was no mention of his act of worship; no altar, no sacrifice initiated by his administration, yet he expected total victory and smooth ride over his challenges. Error!

Suddenly, time was running out. Trouble was brewing for his country. The enemies had rallied their forces. Hell was about to break lose. Do not forget this:

"Jonathan attacked the Philistine governor stationed at Geba (Gibeah). When the Philistines heard the news, they raised the alarm: "The Hebrews are in revolt!"...The word went out all over Israel, "Saul has killed the Philistine governor – drawn first blood! The Philistines are stirred up and mad as hornets!" Summoned, the army came to Saul at Gilgal" (13 vs. 3-4 TM)

So it was our man, Saul, who first called his army together to face the opposition, but at that minute, when he saw what he had come out to face, his strategy for winning the war began to fail. His special advisers had started trading blames amongst themselves. His large cabinet of mostly PDGP loyalists was thrown into confusion and his army of chicken-hearted "boys" became scared to death, running for cover everywhere.

Their momentary victory over President Nahash and his country Ammon was about to become history. Their dream of freedom from Philistine oppression which they had nursed and cherished since their president announced his administration's no-retreat, no-surrender, do-or-die revolution during a nationwide broadcast, probably on that public holiday to celebrate the Ammonite crushing, was about to turn sour. And because His Excellency was the commander in chief who personally led them into the battle, their chief of army or defense staff would have tailed along. And those guys would have become confused along with their commander in chief, and even scared to death with the rest of the army. After all, their commander in chief has become bereft of fresh ideas and strategies for winning the war he called, so what could his lieutenants do?

At that slippery moment of our hero's leadership, just after two years, history records that his "fellow countrymen" started a backward march across the Jordan River, fleeing as refugees into neighboring countries of Gad and Gilead. I have as well witnessed the same in our land where my fellow countrymen, though I am not His Excellency, started crossing over into neighboring countries of Ghana and Gambia and other African countries for economic cover. Forgive my big mouth, but that is the truth. Many have relocated their businesses and companies due to the harsh economic realities in our own land! Although His Excellency still held his ground, and some of his soldiers with him scared to death, yet others could not stand or endure the torment of the anticipation of death. So they began to slip away, right and left.

If you are a keen observer and follower of our country's politics, few months ago before the 2011 general elections, you would have noticed the tension, pressure, and temptation of crossing from one party to another by party members and ill-favored aspirants. This is what political commentators and analysts such as Uzonna Ononye call defection.

Often times, defection is largely caused by the apprehension of losing out or the anticipation of failure in elections amongst party members. You know, everybody wants to identify with success.

But another factor responsible for this is that our people see elections as a time for investments that must yield compulsory turnovers, and so must invest right. Hence, defection becomes necessary. So I can imagine how it was with the people with Saul at that time.

<u>...Doctrine of Necessity</u>

Meanwhile, the greatest prophet of his time; the holy man on whose shoulder rested the destiny of that great kingdom even though he had retired from "active service" had tarried seven days without showing up at the place of national assignment, Gilgal. His Excellency then thought, "What on earth could be keeping this old man from attending to this all-important national assignment...?" Well, too many answers kept flooding his already confused mind but they did not help matters.

As the drama continued, Mr. President suddenly realized of a quick-fix: a formula he had learnt probably from his party chieftains. Call it the "doctrine of necessity", after all, necessity has beckoned, and someone has to respond to it. Maybe his flock of party loyalists reminded him of his powers as the number one citizen; that he should use his veto, after all, sacrifice is sacrifice, and anyone can handle it.

"Mr. President, are you not an anointed of the Lord? So why should you allow one old man, whose overdue retirement you have overlooked for two years now, to hold the entire country to ransom with these challenges breathing down our necks? You had better do something before we wield our impeachment axe and incite the people to withdraw their support for your administration!" they must have threatened.

But our hero tried to maintain his poise; to exercise a little more patience till the holy man would arrive. But then, a look at the other end where his party people were forced him to listen to them; to, at least that once, adopt the doctrine of necessity.

His Excellency saw the huge army of the fearless opposition chanting war songs and marching down with every joule of energy and confidence in them; the whole earth reverberating as they marched towards the meeting point.

Now, ask a politician whose political ambition had once been threatened by the opposition and their moves indicated and implied jeopardy for him, he would tell you that his experience was similar to that of President Saul at that time. Or ask a man who needed urgent assistance to ameliorate his family's poor living condition but all his hope of a better option is being deferred, what he might do with the other options open to him. Doubtless, he could be compelled to follow his head, and not his heart.

However, we all know that such moments in our lives call for maximum caution, as we must not brush aside the standard and expectation of God from us. Such was the scenario our hero found himself in.

As everything played out, Prophet Samuel was also walking down to join His Excellency and the rest of the people at the ground. Probably his age was beginning to tell on him such that he had to maintain a slow but steady pace.

Meanwhile, the Council of Heaven, that's the Heaven's Parliament always and forever chaired by the All-knowing, Almighty God had issued orders to all Angelic Beings in all their ranks not to interfere, so all of them kept their fingers crossed and watched the drama unfold in God's own state. Whether we believe this or not, God has written the script of our lives and He is also the Director of the drama in which all of us are playing one character or the other. If we play according to His direction, things end well for us, but if we decide to direct our lines by ourselves, we may end up not arriving at a happy ending.

Ask any movie director, he would tell you that some casts are tempted to interpret their roles and lines contrary to the director's expectation, and if they are allowed to do that, the movie will not end according to the script unless it's altered. But God will not alter His script. Hence, no one was allowed to interfere.

Finally, the last straw that broke the Carmel's back: the PDGP loyalists began to retreat from their president's side as they saw the opposition grow stronger, coming after them. They broke the oath of allegiance they took while accepting their portfolios at their commissioning.

The men who once sang his praise at the rallies, pledged their undying commitment after his first conquest of President Nahash of Ammon, and encouraged him to engage the greatest challenge of his administration, began to sing a different song at the sight of the challenge which they spurred Mr. President to engage.

May God help all our excellences and all those in authority at all levels even on the home front in Jesus name. May they always seek His face through prayers and waiting on Him before embarking on all their mandatory assignments!

I pray also that they receive the grace to ask for and receive the compulsory wisdom to direct them well in choosing the right people to work in their cabinet, management teams, and advisory boards so that they can successfully carry out their divine mandates. I pray that they will not despise the wisdom of God that's available through consulting with God's true prophets so that they can tread with caution in handling oppositions.

Even a man who wants to marry should embrace the God-factor in order to marry a good and godly wife who would help him in making and running a good and godly home knowing that the home is the beginning of every nation. And the men who are already married should allow God to direct them on whether to involve their wives in making and deciding on very important issues that affect their families' future as well as that of the nation. It is that serious.

So for President Saul and his political party, they did not do their homework very well before rolling out the drums of war against Philistine oppression. They underestimated the challenges facing their country that their preparation ended with the conscription and training of the army without providing the tools to really combat those challenges.

Need I say that the case is no different in our own land where the Police are expected to fight crime and criminals but are not well equipped for the task? Find out: How many helicopters do our police have? How many of the 21st century security gadgets and tools do they have to fight terrorism in our land? In this rich country where even some clerics and civil servants boast of owning private jets, yet the government cannot equip the force well. Each year, the budget on provision of security goes high but at the end, the same story.

Increasing the pay packet of security chiefs and personnel may boost their morale but cannot guarantee that they will work better. This is because it is only a man who is alive that enjoys fat salary and emoluments. If there is a complementary provision of sophisticated security equipment to stop the madness of terrorists and criminals, the policeman you are sending out will be confident to engage these enemies with the hope of staying alive to enjoy the government's largesse. He will not run away from the enemies because he has the latest weapon that can destroy the enemies and their weapons. But that is not the case. So I do not so much blame the police if that has been the reason for their often propagated "incompetence" in combating crime.

If just one Nigerian clergyman can fly and maintain more than one private jet, (this is just one Nigerian out of many others who fly private jets), then all of them, if they are truly patriotic, can give our police and other law enforcement agents more than 200 helicopters within few years! Even the monies, unnecessary wastes, that our governments vote in their budgets for frivolities can give the police force a facelift.

For instance, in the 2012 budget proposal, which the Federal Republic of Nigeria's President tagged "Fiscal Consolidation: Improving Growth and Providing Employment" during his presentation before the Joint Session of the National Assembly, oil production was put at 2.4 billion barrels per day at a benchmark of $70 per barrel.

Then, in the budget, about N5 billion naira was expected to take care of ambassadors' children's school fees and N59 billion for just the salaries of about one thousand staff members of a government agency. And only the Budget Office was to get about N215 million just for refreshment. N150 billion was voted for the National Assembly while the Judiciary would get N85 billion. Indeed, it was a budget of consolidation just for the civil servants! Then, you tell us that you want to end our afflictions and sufferings; that insecurity would become history soon and that corruption would soon leave our borders to God-knows-where. Well, we are waiting.

President Saul thought that equipping his son and himself would make others to follow him to die in the hands of their opposition but he was dead wrong. The army began to retreat fast.

It is saddening to find out that our educated, nay, schooled leaders could not make or draft adequate plans and policies to fight the oppression that has kept our dear people in almost perpetual doldrums. No wonder one of our music legends sang, "Which Way Nigeria?" and the answer our then heroes could give us was the same that President Saul gave: he tried to take charge of the messy situation as they also did. But the result was alarmingly devastating to national progress. Our Book tells us,

"So Saul took charge: 'Bring me the burnt offering and the peace offerings!' He went ahead and sacrificed the burnt offering. No sooner had he done it than Samuel showed up! Saul greeted him" (13:9-10 TM)

<u>Violation of Due Process: A Constitutional Breach</u>

Oh, what a story! His Excellency took charge and went contrary to Chapter Four, Section Three, Sub-section

Ten of their Sovereign Constitution, which is, the Fourth Book of The Law (Numbers) Chapter 3 Verse 10 – the Law of Moses.

Now, this is the problem with most leaders. They fail to take charge when they can still manage and handle the situation. They fail to nip in the bud that which can bring about their fall until their fall becomes inevitable. They do not take certain sections of the law serious by doing what they are expected by law to do until they put themselves in a situation where the temptation to violate other sections of the law becomes tense and extremely difficult to avoid.

So when they fail to act in accordance with lawful expectation and the situation gets out of hand or out of their control, their willingness to obey the law is put to a compulsory test. With their pride put on the line, and in their attempt to save what is left after their probably shameful response, they disregard due process, venture into the forbidden, and end up in more terrible errors. Then, when the ultimate authority – the watchers – show up after their deed is done, they, like Sau, I would begin to greet them.

The King James Version of our most reliable Bible renders verse 10 of chapter 13 of the book of First Samuel thus:

"And it came to pass, that as soon as he had made an end of offering the burnt offering, behold, Samuel came; and Saul went out to meet him, that he might salute him."

The phrase **"salute him"** in the original Hebrew means **"bless him".** That is to say that President Saul went out to bless Samuel immediately he saw him at the scene of that national assignment.

Permit me to say that His Excellency's greeting or salutation or blessing was a product of a guilty conscience; an act to cover his mess. He knew that he had gone contrary to divine ordinance and violated the provisions of their constitution as contained in the Law of Moses, and so wanted to make up by blessing the holy man.

As a matter of fact, he knew the consequence of his act; that the Council of Heaven had been upset and provoked to disappointment, and that his government was now at the mercy of their spokesman Samuel, therefore he quickly, before Samuel could say a word, went out and saluted him. It sounded more like a bribe – to appease the man who had come to register his employer's disappointment – than a salutation or a blessing or a welcome note.

You know that kind of a thing. Someone just excretes on a holy ground in the absence of the priest, and at his sudden, unexpected appearance, the person tries to douse the stinking stench of his abomination with a spray of fragrance.

Similarly too, an honorable or an executive who just committed a national taboo; an act condemnable by law, but in trying to cover up their deed and appease the brazen disappointment and disapproval of their constituency or countrymen, thinks of a smart way out. Some might come up with sponsored media piece or special salutation to hail the senior citizens and elder statesmen of their constituencies or communities for their unflinching support to their leadership. Others still might try to use bogus adverts to showcase their foolishness under the guise of promoting the national dream for national interest.

President Saul did that. He went out, made the first move, attempted to shut the mouth of the holy man; tried to make Heaven's spokesman look the other way. But all his gimmicks did not work on the man who was operating from the supernatural realm where no such practice is given attention or even attempted.

We must note at this juncture that Samuel did not frown at His Excellency's malfeasance just because he was a prophet and Saul was not. He was just a natural man like all of us though he possessed supernatural acumen. But who amongst us does not have a portion of the supernatural or a degree of divinity or an exceptional ability to do something good?

God endowed us from creation but most of us end up brushing aside that nudging of the Spirit to run our lives the way we deem fit to our detriment. Samuel had options. He could have chosen to compromise the ethics and standard of his hallowed office but he chose to uphold its integrity. He could have chosen to ask for a fat settlement by His Excellency to use to appease Heaven's Parliament to overlook Mr. President's error, but he saw it as betrayal of his divine mandate.

After all, history is replete with men in the same office who greedily ran after rewards of men in power to turn blind eyes to the truth. Examples are Prophet Balaam and Judas Iscariot. Even in this contemporary era, many prophets have compromised their office like the two mentioned above not to talk of their counterparts in other leadership climes.

You do not need to be a prophet to say no to corruption. Whatever office you occupy, God created it. He established all faculties of human endeavor for the purpose of establishing righteousness, peace, and joy in the Earth. God by the Act of Heaven's Parliament created this Earth to reflect His true nature and their policies as are practiced in Heaven above. That is why

Jesus Christ said, ***"Thy will be done in the earth as in heaven."***

We are not expected to do otherwise. He who does otherwise is not wise! And because President Saul did otherwise by breaking protocol; violated due process and rubbished the rule of law, the special envoy, Prophet Samuel, who Heaven sent, frowned and heartbrokenly asked, ***"What hast thou done?"***

...What Have You Done?

The same question God asked Mrs. Eve Adam, the very First Lady of the Earth in her exquisite paradise-home. The same question we are now asking our past heroes, "What have you done?" The same question the future generations will ask us, "What have you done?"

What have you done with the office where God magnanimously put you? In other words, what did you do? And what are you doing? What did you do with the opportunity given to you to seek God and His Parliament's blessing in repositioning your community, constituency, and country? What did you do with the opportunities that presented themselves for you to transform the nation?

What did you do with the vast natural and human resources that God in His generosity endowed this country with? What did you do with the opportunity you had to offer acceptable sacrifice to God in preparation for the execution of your divine mandate?

Most of our leaders once given a mandate to lead forget to incorporate God in their schedule only to remember Him when faced with imminent national, organizational, or even a personal disaster or a serious family challenge. In the process, especially when they are not getting His attention, they engage in more serious error-laden activities!

And once they are caught in that web of resulting though unintended consequence, they begin to look for means of rubbing it off on anything which they diplomatically and craftily design. These things have continued down the age right from the first generation heroes of our country and the continent such that the ugly trend has appeared to overwhelm our people. "What hast thou done?" is the question of the moment.

Those who left public office or private companies after years of serving themselves of this country's resources today yell at the top of their voices calling for a drastic move towards nation building. They are now calling on those that succeeded them to work towards the building and development of lasting infrastructures and schemes for national progress. I join the noblest prophet to ask them, "What hast thou done?"

What did you do when you were in that capacity that someone now occupies? As the director of that agency or parastatals, what did you do to ensure the development of those basic structures for national progress that you are now canvasing for? You are now calling for transparency in public office, were you transparent while in office? Even now, are you transparent in that office of an elder statesman you now hold?

You left the government house and decided that the religious house is the place for service after retirement, but if we probe very well, you are no different except that you now do it in the name of God. Since you left that office, is it not your error that has taken hold on the agency and system that your successors have been fighting hard to correct? "What hast thou done?"

Are you not responsible for the corruption that has eaten deep into that organization? Although they still consider you a hero of some sort, yet you cannot now clear the system of the rot and mess your misdeeds caused this land! No matter what you do now, and the campaign you try to launch now against that error, you cannot turn the hand of time.

Remember, the salutation of His Excellency did not achieve its intended objective. The Prophet brushed it aside and confronted him with the question of the moment: What hast thou done? This is why all the schemes and devices of our leaders to cover their errors have not worked well and will never work well. Even when they seem to work out according to their expectations in the short run, at the end, their nakedness will be exposed when the breath of fresh air they seem to be enjoying at the moment turns into a whirlwind. The only scheme that will work is that of outright repentance towards God in obedience to and observation of His sacred laws. This, President Saul did not do. He only stated unwise reasons for his impatience, disobedience, and total disregard for his country's constitution. These were his reasons:

"Because I saw that the people were scattered from me, and that thou comest not within the days appointed, and that the Philistines gathered themselves together at Michmash; Therefore said I, The Philistines will come down now upon me to Gilgal, and I have not made supplication unto the LORD: I forced myself therefore, and offered a burnt offering" (13 vs. 11-12)

Now, if we bullet the reasons this hero gave for his misdeed according to the Message Bible, they will look like this:

❖ *"I saw I was losing my army from under me"* (unanticipated disappointment – a reality of life)

- ❖ **"You** (Samuel) *hadn't come when you said you would"*
- ❖ **"The Philistines were poised at Michmash** (a reality of war)"
- ❖ **"The Philistines are about to come down on me in Gilgal"** (his thought in apprehension and fear)
- ❖ **"I haven't yet come before God asking for his help"** (which he should have done before making the move).   Emphasis mine

In our usual tradition of fairness, let us at least give our hero a benefit of the doubt. We shall equally extend this fairness to all our heroes, past and present, which have had similar reasons for their misdeed, by discussing the reasons as bulleted above.

First, His Excellency was losing his army of followers and supporters from his side so he decided to venture into the error. It is an error of being the man of the people and not the man of God as well.

Every authority beginning from the family which is the smallest unit of a nation to the federal authority of a nation is representing a superior authority. That is why none of these authorities at their various levels can take the laws of the land for granted and go free – they get punished by those over them.

It is most regrettable how often some leaders switch from persistence and consistency in godly living to the popular ungodliness due to a hurried switch of their people's support motivated by an unnecessary fear of the unknown. Leaders who have had similar encounter as that which President Saul had with Prophet Samuel ought to know how to conduct themselves in the face of emergencies and unpredictable circumstances. It is disappointing when such leaders begin to display a sense of insecurity due to the inconsistency of their mortal supporters.

Come to think of it, it was the same army that His Excellency took almost the first two years of his administration to recruit and train that he complained got scattered from him. It then means that all his investment in recruiting and training them was a complete waste of his nation's resources. Have we not witnessed the same here in our land?

Some of our leaders wasted so much investing in projects that did not receive divine approval, and so those projects ended up yielding no positive returns to the country. Meanwhile, huge sums of money from the nation's treasury had been expended uselessly. The only sour benefit we derive today from them is the sight of those abandoned, unsuccessful projects that keep reminding us of the prodigalism of those leaders.

If we begin to list such projects and programs that some of our heroes embarked on without Heaven's backing, we might be short of space and ink to do so. Besides, the inconvenience of doing that is not worth it. It is no use. But those of us who have been closely watching events occurring and re-occurring in the polity and economy in our country and our continent can attest to the fact that foolishness and selfishness in such stupendous investments had characterized the several post-colonial administrations of some of our leaders.

If we are allowed to probe those administrations, we will find from the key players, if they will be honest, that only the projects and programs they properly presented to God in prayers and got His approval recorded success. For others who did otherwise, it was a harvest of failures throughout their regimes.

More so, it was President Saul and his PDGP government that drafted and approved the budget for the force. They also made appropriation for the recruitment and training of his army that later withdrew their allegiance and broke their vow to defend their nation.

If we check very well, maybe, the allocation for the purchase of arms and ammunition was hijacked by the party elders and executives and shared amongst themselves since the efforts to get some for the soldiers proved futile. This action equally annoyed the

Council of Heaven that they moved a motion for the vote of no confidence in Saul's administration.

So it was a political party arrangement that made His Excellency to exclusively and executively exclude God Almighty, The Most Excellent from his government from the very beginning. The defense training program was a complete farce!

In preparation for the 2011 general elections in our country, the agency saddled with the huge task of organizing and executing the program had, prior to registration of voters and the main election, showed readiness for the exercise. With the appointment of Professor Attahiru Jega as the helmsman of the Independent National Electoral Commission, INEC, almost everyone in the country had hailed the Dr. Goodluck Jonathan's administration for taking his electoral reform promise to the next level. As a matter of fact, almost every well-meaning citizen in the country and in the Diaspora endorsed the appointment of the professor who was widely described as a man of integrity and a no-nonsense man.

So when he put in a requisition for money – about N85 billion – for the exercise, everyone called on the lawmakers and the presidency to grant it. Everyone trusted that the no-nonsense professor and his commissioners – all professors as well, would rightly appropriate the lump sum which covered logistics, and the recruitment and training of manpower which included the National Youth Service Corps members used for the exercise.

But during the voters' registration that preceded the main exercise, trails of failure marred the exercise due to various factors. While some blamed the initial poor performance and slow pace of registering eligible voters on the computer systems used for the exercise, others alleged that the NYSC members were not adequately empowered for the exercise. Even though the exercise later picked up at a little faster than a snail's speed, the outcome was almost the same, leaving many eligible voters out of the franchise.

However, if newspaper reports are anything to go by, then the seemingly prevalent opinion that the NYSC members were not adequately trained could be the major reason for the initial hiccup that marred the voter registration. That's the opinion of many especially those in high places.

But my take on it is that both factors, that is, the training of the personnel including the NYSC members on the use of the computers and the computer systems purchased and used were responsible for the voters' registration mess. And to take the responsibility for the mess should be INEC for not utilizing the budget well.

One of the national daily newspapers had on their front page that the Prof lamented that more funds would have made the difference. But I say more funds or not, they did not prepare well for that all-important national exercise. After all, apart from the money released to them by the Federal Government, another newspaper carried news that about US$80 million was released to the body and to other non-governmental organizations (NGOs) by UNDP for the 2011 general elections. That's if we should believe newspaper reports. And why should not we? I did not see anywhere they refuted those reports, so? That means that the cry for more funds by INEC was unnecessary.

Their failure was a case of wrong order of priorities. My opinion: they did not embrace the God-factor right from the start!

Listen: We cannot rule God out of our national existence because whether we know it or not, He has been there looking at us, checking out how we treat His presence and concern about our lives. He is at the centre of life, and most times we go in circles when we could ask Him to direct us how to go about our lives.

But why do we fail to do the simple task of asking Him in? It is because many of our heroes believe that God should not be dragged into our national, state, and local government affairs. They treat God as a bogey man who should only be brought in when unforeseen and unanticipated challenges threaten their mission. That is to say they use God whenever they need Him, and shut Him out whenever they choose. But little would they realize that God cannot be shut out! They do not see God at the centre of the nation, its agencies, commissions, and their operations, but He is there always; He has never left His position.

President Saul should have placed God first in the line of battle against Philistine oppression, and he would not need to fight because with God in the front line, there would be no more oppression; it would have fled the country on its own. But instead, he took up the training of an army that he thought in his calculation would dismantle that opposition. He was wrong!

Likewise, our no-nonsense professor with his prof-commissioners may have relied on his much talked about profile and proficiency, making it the first on the list of factors to decide the outcome of his mission. The electoral body may have plunged into the task though with a careful study and thorough understanding of the terms of references, but without giving much time to really involve the One at the centre right from the start. You know that kind of a thing.

You are the boss, and you call your "boys" at a roundtable and after a three-minute opening prayer, that is, if that was necessary, you begin to address them on the urgency of the hour: "Gentlemen, I believe you understand the task ahead of us, and that we have got what it takes to get it done. Mr. President is not expecting an excuse for failure, but a job well-done. So let us give it to him and make our countrymen and women proud of their beloved country once again. We can handle it, so get moving and get down to business. If you encounter any challenge, dial the headquarters, we will fix it together..." And everyone rushes out of the conference room with some probably making the sign of the cross across their faces to perhaps tell God, "We acknowledge you, Lord". Does that make any sense?

I suppose you have seen that severally in the movies, but they do happen. But let us say that our electoral reformers got God involved and gave Him due acknowledgement, how deep was their reverence? If I were in their position or in that meeting with the boss, a three-day national prayer retreat would have been considered a worthy factor for success before the commencement of recruiting and training of the personnel. What does this do? During this period, the challenges that could mar the exercise would be exposed so that solutions are proffered beforehand.

Churches and mosques may have been asked to pray for the success of the election, but how many really spent quality time in prayer for a peaceful election? They may have prayed but it was not enough and should not have taken the responsibility from the agency in charge of the elections. After all, if an honorable direly needs a special favor from a god, he does not send an envoy to the priest while he goes off on another business. He goes to that priest and makes his request otherwise the gods get angry with him.

Prophet Samuel had been praying for his country and the government yet he requested that His Excellency should take time off his busy schedule to appear before Heaven's Parliament for self-dedication, worship, and sacrifice, and to present his case against the opposition that was threatening his young administration.

If the House of Assembly requests that Mr. President should appear before it, do you think Mr. President would begin to give excuse for not going to appear before the House? Or do you think he would hurry them up during the session when they still have important issues that affect the nation to discuss? Except he wants them to wield their impeachment axe or he wants to lose his second term for contempt of the honorable lawmakers or Contempt of the House.

Prophet Samuel knew the power of personal commitment, self-dedication, and divine covenant but sorry to say, our heroes did not recognize all that. After all they are legends and luminaries; intellectually active, but spiritually passive.

To them, waiting on God for help they already have or can get, and for an assignment they can naturally handle does not make much sense. But ironically, the results they produce usually show that their legendary is adulterated and outrageous nonsense! Vanity and smoke! That was why the prophetic professor, Samuel cautioned the PDGP:

"Be warned: If you live badly, both you and your king (candidate) ***will be thrown out"*** (12 vs. 25 TM) Emphasis mine

Even though the prayer of a prophet can save his land yet the prayer of the entire people of that land will do much more. If the prayer of one man can save so many, then think of what the sincere prayers of all the people can do. That is why God says, ***"If the people that are called by my name shall humble themselves ...and pray...I will answer"***.

In my opinion, the electoral body did not have enough preparation spiritually and in all other areas before and during the general elections, and we all witnessed the outcome. Apart from the voting and counting of votes that were said to be free and fair, the violence that claimed the lives of some NYSC members and others attested to a bad end. May the souls of those that died rest in peace! They were heroes too and would continue to be.

But just imagine what would have happened if our professors had declared a meeting with the Council of Heaven and had invited any of God's prophets whose God-given anointing puts the devil on the run and shuts demons at bay. Honestly, heaven would have touched the earth and all the perpetrators of the pre-election and post-election violence that claimed the precious lives of our patriotic NYSC members and others would have fled this country together with their sponsors. Our heroes should learn from history.

However, I do not altogether blame our INEC professors because they may have done their best – the best they knew how to do. It was the system in which they and their counterparts in other agencies operated that was the problem. It was a system that spent more days campaigning for the support of the people to their excellences and their governments than adequately preparing for the great task ahead.

Looking at and judging from the duration the electoral body had to deliver satisfactory results to the nation, they may have faced a similar challenge that President Saul faced at Gilgal. It was a situation that forced him to abandon ethical procedures and standard, and took the cheapest option open to him. It was a situation that the system birthed for him and put him on the spot that taking the hard way – the only way to attract Heaven's commendation – became foolish in his eyes. So he decided to put "the people" ahead of God and ended up in God's black book.

...<u>The Switch of Allegiance</u>

President Saul should therefore blame himself for doing what he did and getting what he got. Our heroes too should take the blame for the careless loss of lives occurring in our country and the continent.

Second, His Excellency accused his lack of patience on the prophet's delay in attending the national mandate at Gilgal within the seven-day period. Our Book records,

"He waited seven days, the time set by Samuel. Samuel failed to show up at Gilgal, and the soldiers were slipping away, right and left" (13 vs. 8 TM)

I tell you the truth; it was not the delay of the prophet that made His Excellency to do what he was not supposed, by law, to do. He had waited, alright, for seven days **"according to the set time that Samuel had appointed"**, and at the end of the seventh day perhaps, he gave up waiting and took charge.

Suddenly as he stepped into that restricted office which was the exclusive preserve of the priests according to his nation's constitution, Samuel whose office it was showed up! Why did not he wait one minute more, one more hour, or one more day?! Why could not he wait just a little longer?

Why did not it come to his mind that the prophet might just be there any minute since it was the seventh day? Why did not he trust that the holy man would not fail such appointment since it fell within his jurisdiction to carry it out? His Excellency knew the law very well that it was only the priests from the Levites that should handle that aspect of their national life.

Why did not he leave it for them? Ah! Your Excellency, Your Majesty, Your Lordship, Distinguished Lawmaker, Mr. Honorable, Reverend and Most Reverend, etc., why not be patient, trust through, and allow the Most Excellent King, Holy and Reverend God Almighty and His Parliament to go ahead of you?

His Excellency knew that section of the Law that disqualified him from performing the duty of sacrificing that kind of burnt offering. He also knew the consequence of contravening that section. To help us, the section reads:

*"**Then the Lord said to Moses, "Summon the tribe of Levi and present them to Aaron as his assistants. They will follow his instructions and perform the sacred duties at the Tabernacle on behalf of all the people of Israel for they are assigned to him as representatives of all the**"*

people of Israel. They are in charge of all the furnishings and maintenance of the Tabernacle. However, only Aaron and his sons may carry out the duties of the priesthood; anyone else who presumes to assume this office shall be executed" (Numbers 3 vs. 5-10 TLB) Emphasis mine

Public execution was what His Excellency toiled with! The law does not respect any man who does not respect it no matter their nomenclature or title! If you toy with the Law, you toy with your life and toil all your life!

President Saul did not wait, again, he did not learn from history, from the error of his countrymen in their first republic in the Wilderness of Sinai. That generation that God, through Prince Moses, brought out of Egyptian slavery and was taking down to the Promised Land prepared for them. But first, they had to get the Law – the constitution for the new republic; the Law which would guide them in the new state they were going to start to live.

Therefore, Prince Moses their hero, being summoned by Heaven's Parliament, went up to receive that constitution. But because the legislative session took longer than the people anticipated, the people grew tired of waiting. History records,

"And when the people saw that Moses delayed to come down out of the mount, the people gathered themselves together unto Aaron, and said unto him, Up, make us gods, which shall go before us; for as for this Moses, the man that brought us up out of the land of Egypt, we wot not what is become of him" (Exodus 32 vs. 1)

Impatience! This is a vice that has kept many a hero from realizing their mandate and claiming total victory in life. For the nation of Israel that was just about six months old, what was the reason for their impatience? They said, **"As for this Moses, the man that brought us up out of Egypt, we wot not what is become of him"**.

Prior to this sad scene, the man Moses had brought them to Sinai Mountain to meet with God and His Parliament. They had heard the voices of thunder and had seen flashes of lightening as the convoy and entourage of Heaven touched the Mount, but they were sore afraid, and so requested Moses who was used to that to go to God on their behalf (Exodus 20:18-19). Thus, they recognized Moses as the man between them and God; their middle man, their representative. They also recognized him as the man who brought them out of Egyptian captivity, and acknowledged the fact that they needed the guidance of "gods" to get to the Promised Land.

But then, when they were expected to show understanding and gratitude by waiting for further instructions from Heaven's Parliament that ordered their evacuation from the land of captivity, they claimed that they did not know what had become of their helmsman.

How people can easily forget! They forgot that they had mandated him as their Distinguished Representative to hear from God on their behalf. They forgot that they had sworn to wait to hear what God and His Parliament would tell them through Moses to do, and that they had promised to do it.

At the time their patient waiting would have been counted for them as righteousness; when that compulsory period of waiting would have paid off, they realized that they had waited for too long, perhaps longer than necessary. They realized that Moses was probably doing his own business there with Heaven's Parliament and had left them to do theirs. Maybe some had reminded the others that if they should wait any longer for their leader, other people might get to the Promised Land before them and start enjoying the milk and honey flowing in the land. And so they protested.

It was the people's fifth protest within that short period of their independence from Egyptian colonization. It was a protest incited and sponsored by the chiefs and senior citizens of the young nation who felt that their young nation should not be held down in the wilderness by one man who came to them with the preaching of a new kind of government in the name of the Lord. You may ask, "How did I know?" Our Book records that:

When the people saw that Moses delayed..., the people gathered themselves together unto Aaron..."

History has it that about six hundred thousand footmen beside women and children and also beside a mixed multitude who were not Israelites came out of Egypt (Exodus 12). So it was not the entire populace that gathered together unto Aaron even though the entire people may have known that Moses had delayed his coming from the mount. So it was the elders or family and tribal heads that must have incited their colleagues and counterparts to pay the House Speaker, Aaron a visit at his tent – his wilderness quarters – to discuss the state of the nation.

Believe me, it was a party of impatient, unpatriotic, and insecure chieftains that considered themselves honorably and suitably positioned to meddle in the affairs of their nation's leadership that confronted Aaron, the Speaker of the House with the idea of impeaching the Prime Minister, Moses. They had convinced him that though the Prime Minister Moses was his blood brother, he should put sentiments aside and perform his duty as the Speaker; after all, he was the Speaker of the entire nation although God appointed him.

And to get to him easily, they may have commended him for representing them well in the delegation to Pharaoh to release them from Egyptian imprisonment and to grant them independence. Politics did not start today folks; it has been there, and God has always frowned at its maneuvering.

Those confused elders of the people may have also told Aaron that what was important to their young nation was to go forward, so their motion to impeach Moses was done in the best interest of the nation. And they had to do that without the Prime Minister! God help His people! They thought they were going forward but they did not know they were actually moving the nation backward into idolatry and idiocy. You should know the end of those people.

...The Breaking Point

For President Saul, it was the switch of allegiance of his party chieftains and supporters from his government that pressured him into stepping into a hallowed jurisdiction reserved for ordained priests only. What about our own people? It is the same factor that has been responsible for their error of abuse of office.

In the case of N38 billion "misappropriations" brought against former Speaker of the House of Representatives and his deputy in the 6th National Assembly, the high court judges ruled that the accused, that is, the Speaker and the Deputy Speaker had no case to answer as they did not appropriate the loan to themselves.

But the Counsel to the Economic and Financial Crimes Commission, EFCC, Mr. Festus Keyamo had argued that the act of the duo, Bankole and Nafada, was that of usurpation of power not conferred on them. The learned fellow argued that the former Speaker and his deputy had no right, under the provisions of the law and the rules and regulations of the House to do what they did. So it was simply the act of stepping into a jurisdiction that required the consent and approval of the entire House for them to do which they did not fulfil.

Now, I am not a legal practitioner to argue for or against, but with the track record of Mr. Keyamo in the judicial system of our country, I am convinced that he knew what he was arguing. But you know the system we are in; it is such that once the "elders" rule over a matter, like "the law of the Medes and Persians that cannot be changed", they stick to it even when it is an error of judgment.

However, from the standpoint of the law of God contained in our Book – the Bible – the defaulter in those days was liable to face public execution. This is because any attempt to make any form of sacrifice or perform any duties for presumed national progress, which one is not empowered to do by the provisions of the Sovereign Law of God or by the accepted constitution of the sovereign state is an abuse of office, and therefore an error punishable by law!

Whether it is the President, the Vice President, the Senate President, the Speaker of the House, a Governor, or a Director, abuse is abuse, period! Let it be a Bishop, Right Reverend or Most Reverend, His Lordship or His Majesty, a Chief Priest or a Chief Imam that is involved in that abuse, the nomenclature of the culprit does not change the nomenclature of the offence. So it is still an abuse and is punishable by both divine and mortal laws!

God told Prince Moses Amram, the Prime Minister this: ***"However, only Aaron and his sons may carry out the duties of the priesthood; anyone who presumes to assume this office shall be executed."*** (TLB)

No president would be happy to see his vice go about carrying out his executive duties which he did not empower him to do on his behalf. No speaker of the house would want any member of the house to go about functioning in the capacity of the speaker while the speaker has not abdicated the right to his office to him. No royal majesty would be pleased with any member of his royal cabinet who goes from clan to clan announcing one community project or the other to his subjects without his consent. Anyone who presumes to assume another's office should be prosecuted – that was God's stand, and He was serious about it. But not so in my country! Our leaders are not serious about the law!

If we look closely at President Saul's case, it was not the delay of Samuel that pushed him to misbehave; it was the reaction of the people to his seven days of waiting in the face of a predictable collapse of his government. It was the reaction of his loyalists to the length of his patience.

He must have thought, "After all, Samuel is just one man: I can do without him, but I cannot do without my army, my security chiefs, and my party supporters who encouraged me to embark on this fight-to-finish project to end the Philistine oppression on my country." Yes, this may have been his thought, probably after holding an emergency session with his party leaders, close aides, and the who's who in his government. And God was watching His Excellency.

Heaven's Parliament made no comment at the time. It was a moment of testing the faith and patience and loyalty of the man they considered could pull a surprise owing to the fact that he, by himself, would not have smelled that office. It was his defining moment – it comes to every man, to every hero. It was a war of decision that waged in his mind; a very necessary war that must decide the outcome of the real physical war with the enemies. Every hero faces it, and how they handle it determines how the real war will go – whether they will win or lose. For President Saul, he lost it due to popular vote – by listening to voices. It happens in our environment too.

The heavy lobbying by party leaders and loyalists, the strong persuasion by close relatives, and the threats by godfathers to abandon them for other candidates if they do not play by their rules – voices! All these conflict with the inner persuasion to pursue the right course, to keep keeping on despite.

All these decide the depth of a man's conviction, the length of his patience, the breadth of his vision, and the height of his love for God and for his country. Many a heroes fall at this point. Saul was one of them, are you? He could not wait a little longer not because God's Spokesman was not going to come, but because he was afraid of losing the men whose allegiance to his government had actually become doubtful.

Leaders who are not afraid of losing their only eternal contact and relationship with God, but are scared to death of losing their human relations, end up losing everything. Foolishness is the name of the game – penny wise, pound foolish!

I saw an American movie "24" some years back, in which a similar scene played out. President David Palmer was faced with the challenge of making a very tough but delicate decision that could make or mar his government and the long-standing democratic principles on international relations of the United States. It was a case of deciding whether to go to war against the nation that was alleged to sponsor the terrorists who "smuggled in" nuclear weapons to the US. The pressure from the Congress and especially from the Joint Chiefs was so much on him.

So his Chief of Staff, Mike, suggested to him to look at the options on the table, call a meeting, and thereby **"make the Joint Chiefs comfortable"**. David Palmer who was reluctant to consider their options replied Mike, **"My job is not to make the Joint Chiefs comfortable."** Of course, he was right.

Making the service or joint chiefs comfortable or happy by looking at their options which, in summary, decided in favor of a full scale war on a nation based on unproven facts and speculations was not in his job descriptions as Mr. President. The decision of any leader either in the face of a serious challenge or not should be such that at the end, he maintains a conscience void of guilt first in the sight of God, and then, in the sight of godly men. I pray that God will help all leaders everywhere!

Other reasons that President Saul gave were as follow: **"The Philistines were poised at Michmash"**, **"The Philistines are about to come down on me in Gilgal"**, and **"I haven't yet come before God asking for his help"** were after thought: a way to cover his main reason; that he was losing his army from under him. That's right. His main reasons that his army was withdrawing from his side and that Samuel delayed his arrival have been stated. But in trying to convince Samuel of his sincerity, he voiced his presumptions and added more reasons.

Leaders who do not lean on God end up like Saul. They do not lean on God because they do not have an enduring and assuring relationship with Him. They do not have this important relationship because they do not like His ways. They feel that God is slow to respond to emergencies, and only a foolish man feels and thinks that. "Why must we wait for God when we can handle the matter ourselves?" they ask.

Then I ask, "Why saying that you have not yet come before God asking for His help since you can handle it yourself? Why bother God since you can handle it?" One of our great bishops in Nigeria once said that God gave us brains so that we could allow Him to rest. That is right to an extent depending on what he implied. But some people have misused that statement because it was made by a known bishop. Yet God says, **"Call upon me in the day of trouble, and I will deliver you."**

Did God not remember that He gave us brains to think out solutions when He commanded us to call on Him in time of trouble and challenges? The Bible instructs,

"Trust in the LORD with all thine heart (heart, mind, brain)**; and lean not unto thine own** understanding (a function of the brain)**. In all thy ways acknowledge** him (a function of the heart, mind, brain)**, and he shall direct thy paths"** (Proverbs 3 vs. 5-6) Emphasis mine

The wisest president, Solomon saw the dire need and advised us with those lines. We can only heed them if we see the need ourselves and engage God first in all our local, national, and international mandates. Moreover, the degree to which we engage the Council of Heaven will determine the degree of their involvement and the level of their response to our affairs. But if we continue to misconstrue the statement of that bishop (if what he meant is what I think), we will continue to reap a fat harvest of failures in our individual life and our national existence!

President Saul did not put God first. If we look at the order of the reasons for his foolish act again, "I have not made supplication unto the LORD" came last. History puts it again:

"And Samuel said, What hast thou done? And Saul said, **¹***Because I saw that the people*** (loyalists, soldiers, party supporters, godfathers, family and friends) *were scattered from me, and* **²***that thou camest not within*** (or before) *the days appointed, and* **³***that the Philistines*** (the opposition, oppression and challenges trying to frustrate my government) *gathered themselves together at Michmash: Therefore said I,* **⁴***The Philistines will come down now upon me to Gilgal*** (which of course never happened)*, and* **⁵***I have not made supplication unto the LORD*** (which he should have done first). *I forced myself therefore, and offered a burnt offering* (a foolish thing he should not have done)" Emphasis mine

You see that? His desire to seek God's help through worship and personal sacrifice came last in the order of factors that led to his action.

If we are permitted to put some of our past heroes on the spot, in the position Saul found himself before Samuel at the time, we might get similar lines from them. Let us not go far back into history to the first republic. We can establish some points with not-too-old events that we all can easily remember, and I mean this without any form of prejudice.

In 1992, for instance, the nation got heated up with the preparations for another military to civilian government elections to be held June of the following year. Finally, it was a battle of the titans between the Social Democratic Party, SDP and the National Republican Convention, NRC with Chief Moshood Kashimawo Olawale Abiola (MKO) and Alhaji Bashir Tofa respectively as flag bearers.

The battle was set and the elections began. The political will of the people was again put to the test and the political wind was blowing, and it appeared that both were favoring the SDP at the time. The Electoral Umpire, NEC, with a Humphrey Nwosu as their chief was poised to declare the reports as the climate showed it. But our gap-toothed handsome General, who had promised a free and fair exercise with an unbiased oversight of that compulsory process was, however, set to do his thing the military way.

Just like Saul, the pressure was on him from different quarters, which was quite expected in such a defining moment in the history of a great nation as ours.

Quite in a dramatic way, defying all the odds that were against him, Mr. Nwosu dared the junta and gave the reports available to him; the reports which, of course, indicated that the Social Democratic Party, SDP was poised to clear the table.

Then, our own General, the man who, as it appeared, had the ball in his court (I heard they called him "The Maradona") took charge, stepped into the office of the Electoral Umpire, and cancelled, nay, annulled the widely acclaimed freest and fairest general polls in the political history of the giant of Africa.

And when the Samuels – the watchers – of his time frowned and asked, "What hast thou done?" he, like President Saul, gave his reasons. Please, avail me the honor of predicting the probable and unpublished reasons he gave as thus:

"Because the results of the elections started coming in too quickly from the South and the returning officers from the North delayed to show up within the time appointed. The wind of victory and the sound of victory came blowing from the South-West instead of from the North-East, as streams of water should flow from top (North) to bottom (South), but the reverse is now the case. Then said I, The Social Democrats will now take over the mantle, and I have not yet consulted with my lords and elders whose interests I have been serving to know what they think about the unanticipated outcome. I forced myself therefore and sacrificed the true election results on the altar of annulment."

Sounds like that.

This is democracy, and constitutionally, I am entitled to my opinion; to say things the way I see them, and the way the Spirit of God inspires me to put them without prejudice or sentiments.

Then, the error led to other sacrifices such as the brutally maiming and claiming of the lives of protesters especially in Lagos as armored tanks and fiery-looking soldiers littered the Centre of Excellence to quell the protests. After all, sacrifice is sacrifice, they would say. Life goes on.

But the Council of Heaven would not overlook such anti-human acts. So they swiftly gave their verdict and sent their representatives who made sure the chief actor on that political stage, our handsome General stepped down or aside – whichever comes first, and that he must never step up again. So it happened and will ever remain – the decree of God-of-the-Angel-Armies. Selah!

Other examples abound but I think the one given above is worth the mention above all else and therefore should suffice. The error of not involving Heaven's Parliament and of not waiting on God is very dangerous.

Meanwhile, at the beginning of his political career, during the time of preparation for the presidency under the guidance of Samuel, Saul behaved himself wisely and godly. It was probably because he had not yet been confirmed and had not moved into the presidential villa, and "the people" had not started showing up in his government, so he was alone with God and Samuel.

But now that he thought he had arrived, and those people began to show up at the villa; some coming with congratulatory and goodwill messages and demanding some attention, he began to act unwisely and ungodly. Then he realized that they were very important to his government while putting God and His Cabinet last.

The people began to tell him how they gathered themselves, met Samuel at Ramah, and requested for the government that produced him as Mr. President. They began to tell him that right from the beginning, they had a stake in the administration of the state. Maybe in the course of their showing up in their batches under different auspices and umbrellas, they began to inform or remind him of the consequences of excluding them or of not recognizing them in the administration of the state. Before you know it, the once goodly man begins to fumble and fall and finally fail the country.

I heard someone say that there were (may be there still are) banana peels on the floor of the National Assembly that have made it almost impossible for our honorable lawmakers to stand firm without compromising integrity. That was what someone actually said at the beginning of our democracy when the impeachment axe was flying all over and some lawmakers could not withstand it.

Out of curiosity, could there also have been banana peels at Aso Rock presidential villa that have been responsible for the repeated falls of our excellences over the years? Maybe there could also be banana peels in all states houses of assemblies, government agencies and parastatal, private companies, and even religious houses that make some of our leaders and potential heroes to stagger and fall into diverse regrettable acts such as we have been discussing.

If so, those banana peels are there because those saddled with the duty of sweeping them away have turned blind eyes. This is because either they have been paid to pretend they are blind or they are actually benefitting well from the fall of our heroes.

My prayer for such privileged few is that God should strike their conscience and stir up their hearts to immediately wake up and respond to the impulses of the Holy Spirit, and remove those "banana peels" now. I also pray that they begin to show that they are not really blind before they go completely and permanently blind, and those whose wages come from the fall of others should look for honorable work to earn honest wages.

So it was when the people-factor took over that our hero began to consider men first before God. When our leaders started neglecting the words of our prophets, things began to fall apart in the country and the continent. And when things fall apart, according to Chinua Achebe, the centre can no longer hold. Unfortunately, it is the good people of the country who suffer the consequences of the disintegration and devastation.

President Saul disobeyed the voice of the prophet and the voice of God, and the following lines became the verdict:

"And Samuel said to Saul, Thou hast done foolishly! Thou hast not kept the commandment of the LORD thy God, which he commanded thee: for now would the LORD have established thy kingdom upon Israel forever. But now thy kingdom shall not continue: the LORD hath sought him a man after his own heart, and the LORD hath commanded him to be captain over his people, because thou hast not kept that which the LORD commanded thee" (13 vs. 13-14)

Note the words, ***"thy kingdom shall not continue"***. That means his right to rule over his country has been terminated. Now, it did not say, "thy kingship shall not continue", but that his kingdom shall not continue.

There is a big difference between kingship and kingdom. While kingship talks about the official position of a king or a ruler or the period of his rule, kingdom talks about the geographical area or country over which a ruler has complete control. So, God just took away the control of the nation from President Saul even though He allowed him to run his full tenure. The kingship was not immediately taken from him but the kingdom was taken. And because it was so, he failed to reason well and to arrest the error that took the kingdom from him. This is what informs the attitude of most leaders to their responsibility.

Just because they are left temporarily in their official capacity even in their error, they care less of the kingdom that is taken away from them. That is why they lose control of their country, constituency, or community although they are still in office. They make laws but some other people take the laws in their hands. And because the control has been taken from them, they cannot fully enforce the law neither can they prosecute those who take the laws for granted. That's why the much sponsored, advertised, and broadcasted rule of law reinvigorated by the late President Umaru Musa Yar'Adua of the Federal Republic of Nigeria remained a delusion.

President Saul failed in keeping the constitution and the verdict was that he would no longer call the shots as his people would not keep his commands.

Losing the kingdom is synonymous with losing the respect of the people of that kingdom to the extent that even stakeholders in the economy and the polity would not respect the laws or the constitution of their country. It is obvious, is it not? There has been no successful government in this land since independence because our heroes and leaders at various capacities have been failing to keep their part of the deal. They have always gone ahead of God, neglected His prophets, and honored their godfathers and party loyalists, and they lost the kingdom. The kingship, though, they retained, but the kingdom – the ultimate divine power to make positive things to happen, they lost. The divine power to triumph over daring national challenges and to enthrone prosperity in godliness in the land, they did not have because they lost the kingdom.

The godfathers may ensure the retaining of the kingship for a while, but only God the Father can ensure the establishment and continuity of the kingdom. The godfathers may ensure retaining the capacity, but only God the Father ensures and guarantees the capability to run the kingdom. The godfathers may ensure that erring leaders stay in office till the end of their tenure, but only God the Father can ensure that the tenure of obedient leaders record significant success and tremendous achievement.

President Saul, no doubt, retained the kingship for a while, but lost the kingdom! That's why he never succeeded in completely defeating the Philistines nor did he end their oppression – the main opposition to his government, and thus, he ended his political and military career woefully in a battle with them on Mount Gilboa. He was consecrated and commissioned at Gilgal, but he was conquered and commiserated with at Gilboa. He began his leadership with God at Gibeah and Gilgal, but ended without God at Gilboa!

Even though he had his preparation for the number one seat of his country in the ways of God guided by the number one prophet of God in his country, yet that did not guarantee his finishing well and strong. This is because he brushed aside all that he learnt and decided to enroll for and walk by the counsel of mere men – the people of his party, the People's Disobedience to God Party (PDGP).

His Excellency hired men, recruited, and trained some of them who could not stand with him through thick and thin. So when he found out they were walking away from him; that they had threatened to switch allegiance if he did not do what they believed was necessary to win the war, he quickly danced to their rhythm. Hence, he ventured into a foolish act – a constitutional breach that eventually and consequently ended his dynasty and enshrined his name perpetually in God's black book. God and His Parliament immediately announced his replacement with a man after God's heart.

To announce the replacement of any leader while he is still in office is considered an announcement of no confidence in that leader. For Saul, his replacement was a man after God's heart; a man who many years later, after having learnt from the error of his predecessor wrote:

"Blessed is the man that walketh not in the counsel of the ungodly, nor standeth in the way of sinners, nor sitteth in the seat of the scornful. But his delight is in the law of the LORD; and in his law doth meditate day and night. And he shall be like a tree planted by the rivers of water, that bringeth forth his fruit in his season; his leaf also shall not wither; and whatsoever he doeth shall prosper" (Psalm 1)

Any leader who wants to prosper in whatever good they're doing; any man or woman who desires to be a hero whose footprints on the sands of history would inspire and not perspire generations after must let those words of President David the Psalmist have a permanent place in their heads and hearts. They must let those words simmer, settle, and saturate their innermost selves to bear fruits of righteousness. God help His people in Jesus' name – amen.

CHAPTER THREE

LOST KINGDOM

The Error of Partial Obedience

The first error of our hero here is mainly that of impatience that led to outright disobedience to the commandment of the Lord. The second however is almost the same as the first except that it was a partial obedience. Nonetheless, they are the same in the eyes of God because outright disobedience and partial obedience are both evil and they result in undermining the power of God and His word.

The first time, Prophet Samuel had told His Excellency to wait seven days for the dedication sacrifice that would guarantee smooth sail over the main opposition and challenges to his government. It was the sacrifice that only the priests according to the Law were allowed to perform for it to be acceptable to God. But Mr. President foolishly and impatiently veered into that hallowed office and ended up losing his kingdom. This time around, a specific instruction came straight from God and His Parliament through their Representative, Samuel. It was an order from the Supreme Court of Heaven after a very long period of jurisprudence against the enemies of God and His country.

"Now go and smite Amalek, and utterly destroy all that they have, spare them not; but slay both man and woman, infant and suckling, ox and sheep, camel and ass" (15 vs. 3)

Before this line of instruction came, the prophet came to the president with words that should communicate the urgency of the hour and the seriousness of the operation. Our reliable Book reveals,

"Samuel also said unto Saul, The LORD sent me to anoint thee to be king over his people, over Israel: now therefore hearken thou unto the voice of the words of the LORD. Thus saith the LORD of hosts, I remember that which Amalek did to Israel, how he laid wait for him the way when he came up from Egypt. Now go and smite Amalek..." (15 vs. 1-3a)

...Permission for Second Term

"Samuel also said unto Saul" means that a first message had been given; something had been previously said to His Excellency, and it was a message from the Lord of hosts. It then means that Heaven's Parliament had looked into President Saul's case and decided to give him a second chance to prove himself a loyal servant-leader. He messed up the first chance when he could not wait for the right jurisdiction to execute a national mandate that beckoned for urgency but required caution.

At the first instance, His Excellency failed the test of patience. He failed to realize that God and His Parliament have the interest of every nation at heart and therefore do not respond or report late for national duty. After all, the Bible says they are "his (God's) people", not the president's people. God knows the end from the beginning, and so knows the best and right time to step in.

Remember that God chose him from the most insignificant clan of macho men, from the smallest tribe of his country. And that choice was made in fulfilment of prophecy which was given by Prophet Balaam in Numbers chapter twenty-four, verses seven and eight about the destruction of President Agag and his people. Two tribes were figuratively mentioned in that prophecy that would lead the operation at the time of fulfilment: Judah and Benjamin, just as Jacob their ancestor spoke about them. But since Heaven decided that the president should come from Benjamin, the lot fell on Saul to fulfil the age-long prophecy.

Although President Saul's excuses and strong reasons for failing his first test were not accepted, yet Heaven's Parliament was lenient to give him a second chance.

I strongly believe in the doctrine of second chance even though not everybody does. And not everybody gets it. From the scriptures, there are strong indications that

President Saul tried to show that he was committed to keeping faith; that he was ready to keep his office by following due process and the rule of law. Yes, he tried to amend his ways after his first error when Samuel left him at Gilgal to face the war he started without the backing of Heaven.

History revealed that his heir-apparent, Jonathan who drew the first blood by killing the Philistine governor at Gibeah went ahead with his troops into the enemies' camp and launched an assault. While His Excellency was regrouping, the battle had already begun and in the process, the people sinned against God by eating animal flesh with the blood!

History further revealed that Mr. President who was commander in chief of the army stopped the people, moved to prosecute the transgressors according to the Law and for the very first time in his regime as head of state, built an altar unto God. A personal effort he never made in years! He was then poised to go down on the Philistines but remembered he could remedy his first error by asking God for help.

However, history further revealed that God did not answer him that day. Perhaps it was this effort at correcting his first act of foolishness that God saw and decided to forward his matter to His Parliament for reconsideration. Finally, a second chance was given.

Praise God! The second chance came. I pray it always comes.

Quite frankly, not all live to get a second chance. Somehow, it comes in different ways. Not everyone survives the aftermath of their first error to get another shot at correcting them and regaining lost glory and worth. You know, it is good to always make a very good, positive first impression because there may not be a second chance to make a good first impression.

Some of our leaders at one time or the other wanted a second chance to probably deliver good governance to their people but the people refused them the opportunity. One of our army generals who after failing to deliver well in his first mandate as head of state and was coerced to "step aside" from office years ago suddenly remembered there was something he did not set right at the villa. But it was too late for him. No second chance was given him.

Another General too who was actually ousted by the one who stepped aside had recently tried to secure a second chance ticket to return to the more glorious villa, but he was considered unfit may be because of the political platform he stood on to "beg" for the ticket. Just like Esau of old, he got a consolatory second position behind a much-favored Goodluck. However, the consolatory second position was not good enough to earn him the much-craved ticket to Aso Rock even though he sought it with tears. What a pity, he did not have a good luck. "Please try again", promotion usually advise.

His case reminds me of my days in the primary school. Any term I came second or third in examination in my class, I would sulk and sometimes cry because I was, most of the time, coming first in my class. Even though my grandmother would still be proud of me, and my parents too, and no one would scold me for coming second, I still did not like it. I am sure no one does. So I do not scold our handsome, gap-toothed General for weeping publicly when he lost to the Otuoke-born Goodluck. I guess his weeping was to show the pain of not getting a second chance when President Saul got his. Well, that's for the generals who had a first chance at the topmost job in the country.

For others who sought to secure a second chance ticket but could not include former Speaker of the House of Representatives in the 6th National Assembly, who after losing out was even arraigned by the eagle-eyed anti-corruption agency, the Economic and Financial Crimes Commission, EFCC, for allegedly misplacing or misappropriating about N38 billion loan.

Others included the former governors of Imo and Oyo states who had, as usual, devised countless strategies to pull wool over the eyes of their people, but did not succeed. Even with support of their godfathers, and in spite of their time-tested gimmicks, thanks to the ruling party, God the Father through His good people denied them the much wanted second chance.

So, for those who, like President Saul, got a second chance, they should count themselves blessed and even privileged, but that is not to say that they have escaped the fate that befell those who did not qualify for the second chance. The Holy history Book cautions,

"If we give up and turn our backs on all we have learned, all we have been given, all the truth we now know, ...and are left on our own to face the Judgment – and a mighty fierce judgment it will be!...This is no light matter. God has warned us that he'll hold us to account and make us pay...Nobody's getting by with anything, believe me" (Hebrews 10 vs. 26-31 TM)

So those who have secured a second chance at whatever positions in any leadership environment even on the home front should not trifle with it otherwise, the spirit of the law they swore to uphold will hunt them until they ultimately pay for it.

...Abuse of Second Term

Indeed President Saul got a second chance but he abused it again! Our Book reveals,

"Samuel said to Saul, 'God sent me to anoint you king over his people, Israel. Now listen again (second chance) *to what God says. This is the God-of-the-Angel-Armies speaking...Go to war against Amalek. Put everything connected with Amalek under a holy ban. And no exceptions! This is to be total destruction – men and women, children and infants, cattle and sheep, camels and donkeys – the works. Then Saul went after Amalek; He captured Agag, king of Amalek, alive. Everyone else was killed under the terms of the holy ban. Saul and the army made an exception for Agag, and for the choice sheep and cattle. They did not include them under the terms of the holy ban. But all the rest, which nobody wanted anyway, they destroyed as decreed by the holy ban. Then God spoke to Samuel: 'I am sorry I ever made Saul king. He has turned his back on me. He refuses to do what I tell him'"* (15 vs. 1-3, 7-10 TM)

What an absurd way to treat the second chance! What a terrible error proceeding from the leader!

God was specific. The message was straight-to-the-point: **"Go to war against Amalek. Put everything connected with Amalek under a holy ban. And no exceptions!"** Yet our hero did otherwise. He suddenly realized that some of the people and the things were too good to be put under the holy ban. But before he went down on Amalek, he did not argue or object to any section of the terms – he simply went. This is partial obedience.

But right there on the field of operation and execution, he began to reconsider the terms of the ban. "How can I destroy all these beautiful beasts and fat farm animals that can serve some good purpose back home? Did God really mean what He commanded – total destruction? What if we save a few of them for sacrifice of thanksgiving to God back home? What if we employ another doctrine of necessity in this instance?" The same scenario that played out at Gilgal repeated itself. Questions filled his mind and he knew their one and only answer: Do as the God-of-the-Angel-Armies had commanded. But he brushed it aside in order to get a logical conclusion that would justify his action.

Many a leader or potential leader have come to this point where clear instructions from a higher authority stand in sharp contrast to their long-held rational belief or tradition. Some of these people and leaders, understanding the weight of hierarchy, submit to the command of their superiors, while others in an attempt to take charge and please their team of followers and also feed their selfish ego, assume responsibility, and force themselves to go contrary to those instructions.

They often feel that as the commander in chief, senate leader or president, house speaker, director-general, honorable minister, executive governor, honorable chairman, his royal majesty, etc., no one in their constituency would dare confront them over compromising the terms and conditions or code of conduct.

In this part of the world where the people have been told and taught even at home and in religious houses to mind only their own business and not to talk about their leaders' mistakes, nay, errors, it becomes increasingly difficult to scold any erring officers.

Even parents forbid their children from pointing out to them areas of parental weaknesses and failures, and so the children grow up with the belief that the failure of their parents is a normal way of life for all parents. This is such that they themselves grow up to continue with the tradition at a higher level, and the negative cycle continues from generation to generation.

Meanwhile, the Holy Bible from where these folks quote is replete with instances where mortal men confronted even the Almighty God with the reality of the moment and with the aftermath of His intended actions.

Examples that readily come to mind are the cases of Moses and Abraham during the wilderness journey to the Promised Land and the pre-judgment of Sodom and Gomorrah respectively. In summary, Moses and

Abraham had told God and His Parliament to think twice about their proposed destruction of their people citing that some good could still be found among them, and God did think twice and calmed down.

But our leaders said that no one should dare discuss them, talk about them, or even point out their failures to them. Well, we are doing just the opposite right now because we have been commissioned to do so, and thank God, it is not a constitutional breach for us to do so. So His Excellency thought he, as the commander in chief, could do as he and his political movement wished, but again, he was wrong.

Although the Representative of Heaven's Parliament was not there at Amalek, yet he got the news of His Excellency's malfeasance even before the local press could probably get it. God was there at Amalek; He went there ahead of our hero to check things out. The Council of Heaven were there. They had seen the fat cattle and choice sheep, yet had commanded total destruction – a just judgment on a sin-wrecked nation. It was judgment against corruption.

History captured the real intention of God when it said, ***"This is to be total destruction – men and women... – the works."*** The activities that were going on among those people at that time were a nuisance before Heaven. The life of the people of that nation was corrupt in the eyes of our Holy God and His Incorruptible Council, so "the works" should be totally destroyed.

Besides, it was a judgment Heaven had waited for ages to carry out on the enemies of God's country because they took advantage of the weakness of His people who just came out of Egypt and dealt cruelly with them. But our heroes saw otherwise: "Let the works stay, destroy only the badly corrupted ones and keep the slightly corrupted as long as they still can serve some good purpose."

Just like our own heroes, when they told us in the name of the Lord that they were out to fight corruption, they did not tell us how they were going to precisely fight that war. Some of them declared War Against Indiscipline; War Against Indiscipline and Corruption, but after their regimes, indiscipline and corruption among their rank and file grew stronger and developed harder shell almost impossible to break.

Others declared and launched several other campaigns to reform and transform, rebrand and reposition the already corrupt system yet the various probe panels and committees of enquiry set up by them had revealed the moral low per cent of the campaigners. Their programs and campaigns failed not because they were not good designs and concepts, but because some corrupt top-notch of the society were not included under the terms of the ban! Yes, they did not include some highly placed people in the list of those to be probed, probably prosecuted, and perhaps put in prison! Yet, Heaven's Parliament was watching.

God saw everything that went down in Amalek, and He has watching everything that's going on in our lands. No one can shut Him out. No technology can shut Him out of Aso Rock, Apo Quarters, or even the White House. When He appoints a man as overseer of His heritage, He has always there as the General Overseer. When He assigns a special duty to someone, He goes ahead of him to specially monitor its execution.

Samuel, God's spokesman, was not there. He did not send any pressman or correspondent to cover the Amalek operation. God was there Himself, and He did the reporting. He told Samuel what went down at Amalek; that the man He gave a second chance failed to live up to expectation. President Saul was not conscious of the presence of God and the representation of His Parliament at Amalek. He was not conscious of the fact that even angels could be sent to do undercover for Heaven's Parliament, (you know the famous FBI stuff) because he was blinded by self and greed for carnal things. And this has been one of the numerous undoing of our own heroes – past and present.

Some of them lack the wisdom necessary for the execution of divine mandates. They also do not have the consciousness of God's presence in their offices probably because they feel that God is too busy with answering the prayers of the masses to concern Himself with the affairs of the state. After all, He has not a politician and is not invited so why would He meddle with earthly governance. Well, God does not meddle; He has at the centre of our whole affairs, He has in charge!

Closed door sessions cannot bar Him even if all pressmen are barred from the sessions. Jesus Christ the greatest leader of all times who manages Heaven and Earth marvelously said in one of His public addresses that nothing can be hidden or be concealed forever. He said that anything done behind closed doors shall be made public someday.

His Excellency might have paid the local press of his day not to report on the Amalek operation. He might have also promised some editors-in-chief and other notable ones political appointments in his next cabinet reshuffle if they would report that he meticulously and religiously executed the Operation No Exceptions (ONE) in Amalek. And probably, they did just that. Unpatriotic press! And trust the watchdogs, the news headlines must have read, "Operation No Exceptions: General Saul the Hero!" or any other captivating caption such as "President Saul: The Hero at Amalek Operation" that could convince any uninformed opposition of His Excellency's commitment to national mandate.

The president and his PDGP must have sealed the mouth of potential harbingers around the country of Amalek with enough *egunje* ('bribe' in our local parlance) in order to kill the details of the Amalek transgression. They might also have raised the wages and allowances of the army chiefs and their lieutenants, and they probably increased the army's annual allocation to convince them of the rationality of saving the healthy loot in the name of national interest, and to buy their loyalty permanently.

These erring folks might have approached the weak opposition parties with diplomatic promises of conceding few seats to them in the next term or cabinet if they could only chorus 'Hallelujah!' to their 'Praise the Lord!' Politics is the name of the game. Think fast, work smart, they would say. If you cannot beat them, then you join them. And the nation goes to ruin.

The PDGP and their president might have shared some Ghana-Must-Go bags of money to all their party legislators in both the upper and the lower legislative chambers, and to all their party executives. This, they must have done to secure a distinction score for Mr. President for the Amalek operation.

Moreover, when His Excellency brought in President Agag of Amalek who should have died a long time in the war, he must have settled the immigration chiefs and other key officials of the service to cover up any traces of his smuggling into the country. He might as well have instructed them to report it as a seized contraband which the presidency was worried about and so was interested in.

Moreover, he must have warned that they must not reveal the true nature of the "goods" in the container as some daring, ambitious journalists might use the information to sell their career.

I remember that it was reported in the news some years ago how an ex-Liberian warlord was "smuggled" into our shores when he was fleeing from Nemesis that hunted him. Even with all the 'smuggling' and concealing of the "goods", Nemesis later caught him and handed him to the No-Mercies where he was in dock at the world's highest criminal court explaining his role in his country's civil war that crippled her economy for years. These were the things our heroes did from dispensation to dispensation. But God looked down, saw everything, and reported accordingly. The report came straight to Samuel who could not be shut up.

The God that cannot be shut out always has men and women who cannot be shut up! Prophet Samuel was one of them. Elijah was another, and in this country there are people like them in both the ecclesiastical and non-ecclesiastical circles.

No matter the degree of corruption in our lands; no matter the height of disobedience to divine commands by our leaders and countrymen, I know there are still men who cannot compromise their righteous positions. If Heaven's Parliament could spot out and report 7,000 people who never yet bowed to nor kissed Baal in the days of Prophet Elijah, then there could be men like them in our lands in our days.

If God could have 7,000 clean men when Baalism was the major corruption that invaded and ravaged the system, and damaged the people's lives and relationship with God, and Elijah thought and concluded he was the last man standing, then it's no gainsaying that God can find men who would speak for Him as Samuel did. My prayer always is that in the day Heaven's Parliament will receive a list of ambassadorial nominees or nominations for other honorary considerations from the President of the Universe, my name will be right on that list. Can God find you the instrument to use to confront the obvious irregularities and anomalies in our lands? Can God confide in you as

He confided in Samuel and is still doing with some people right now?

<u>Report of Heaven's Parliament</u>

Meanwhile, God wired His Amalek report to Samuel and the holy man went. God had already registered His regrets for endorsing the candidacy of President Saul. The details were given to the prophet to deliver as a message to His Excellency at his villa. But the message came to Samuel as a shock. What did he do? The Bible records,

"Then came the word of the LORD unto Samuel saying, It repenteth me that I have set up Saul to be king: for he is turned back from following me, and hath not performed my commandments. And it grieved Samuel; and he cried unto the LORD all night" (15 vs. 10-11)

I remember the late "Senior Advocate of the Masses", Gani Fahwehinmi, SAN. In one of his interviews with the press in his house while recuperating from the last illness before his final passing on, he was shedding hot tears as he lamented the poor state of the nation. He also reiterated his burning desire to see our country in a better state, in better managing hands. In his days, Gani Fahwehinmi, SAN, was a man like Samuel who wept for the things he saw and heard – errors that resulted from bad leadership; the leadership similar in many ways to that of the People's Disobedience to God

Party of Saul's time. But it does not end in shedding hot tears either all day or all night.

When God reports or reveals any disturbing development happening in the state to the people He believes should respond immediately, they should not only respond in praying or crying unto God all night or all day. They should wade in and proffer solutions as would be guided by God.

One of the solutions is for those men to rise up collectively and condemn such unhealthy development; remind the characters behind it of its devastating effect on the state; remind them of the imminent and inevitable consequences on everyone from generation to generation. Gani Fahwehinmi did that. Samuel did the same. Then our Book told us,

"And when Samuel rose early — in the morning ... came to Saul... Saul said unto him, Blessed be thou of the LORD: I have performed the commandment of the LORD" (15 vs. 12-13)

The Preacher, President Solomon who authored the book "Ecclesiastes" said, *"Again I considered all..., then I returned, and saw vanity under the sun."*

Like Solomon, I have seen things. I have pondered over and wondered at so many things; I have considered all and my take on all of these things is that villains are often the first to be crowned heroes either by themselves or their self-acclaimed godfathers. They often fool themselves by blowing their coarse trumpets even when the sound is offensive to tried ears. That was what President Saul did. "Praise the Lord, I have done as I pledged to my country!" "Yes, I did it just as I was commanded, Hallelujah!"

It was the same thing he did at the scene of the first error – he saluted Samuel. A second chance or second term was given to him, but he blew it and came saluting the Honorable Representative of Heaven's Parliament expecting him to fall in line. What a deception!

I saw a very beautiful, creative but revealing cartoon in a particular national daily some time ago that attracted my attention. In that cartoon, a man, possibly a politician, was dusting a book from his bookshelf titled **"How to Make Election Promises and Fail"** while another man, probably a neighbor or partner watched him. Perhaps there are books like that – not published for the general public, but for those who take delight in breaking their pledge and oath to serve their fatherlands.

These people have often seemed to be on the winning side maybe in the ruling political movements and parties except that their victories have never always endured. President Saul, in my judgment, was one of them. He tried to use the first pattern of deceit and gimmick on the man of God but it did not work. He was not even ashamed of such a detestable practice; after all, it has almost become a part of their manifesto to celebrate errors.

Just like it happens on this side, his associates and godfathers would be pleased he brings home the dividends of the mandate they unanimously gave him. They would also sing the usual "For he has a jolly good fellow" for him at a special diner organized to celebrate the so-claimed success of the operation.

So for Saul, why would he not happily salute the prophet who anointed and swore him in as Mr. President? If the executives, the legislators, the judiciary, some spoilt clergy, and his party men have called him a jolly good fellow, why would the prophet be different? This is very worrisome. It is catastrophically worrisome that we are faced with these anomalies. Yet many are not worried. Very sad.

<u>A Lavish Religious Production</u>

Permit us please. I do not know if we have commented on this before in this book series, I mean how disappointing it was for some of us on this other side of the divide but it's painful for us to be reminded of incidents like this one we are now talking about.

A certain political stalwart who served a prison sentence for embezzling, or fairer still, misappropriating millions of naira public funds was celebrated by his political party on his release from prison. And to "cremate" him, a church thanksgiving service was held for him.

Now, what was the celebration all about? That God did not allow him to die in prison? Please, we are being curious here. For how long in prison? Or that those who jailed him – a national duty they were bound by oath to perform – had been shamed since he got out alive? Or that he was alive to enjoy the fruits of his labor, nay, fruits of his error?

So what's the thanksgiving for? That God be praised that a man who disappointed Heaven's Parliament that put him in the prestigious saddle which he turned into a seat of corruption and betrayed that divine appointment was alive to continue to promote the "ideals" of his ruling party? That he was alive to promote the ideals that enthrone lavish extravagance on frivolities and political escapade, and the neglect of godly ethos and etiquettes?

We do not condemn the idea of a thanksgiving service nor do we condemn the priest that officiated it, but for what use? If it were for the reasons mentioned above, then God help His Church and His people!

Why can our heroes not learn from President David Jesse who broke down in tears when confronted by Prophet Nathan for orchestrating the first degree, gruesome murder of innocent Uriah the Hittite and stealing his wife Bathsheba? Why can they not learn from the prodigal son who repented, turned back to his father, and asked for nothing but an opportunity to make up for his prodigalism? Instead, his political party rolled out drums to celebrate, and to pull wool over the eyes of the general public under the guise of thanksgiving.

If I were the principal character that was celebrated, I would invite my party to come thank God for giving me a second chance at life; to be a better citizen and a true patriot. And that would not require a fun fare! It would have been a moment for sober reflection and for asking my country and her good people to forgive me while I take my time to plan a glorious comeback to the path of honor and the stage of moving the country forward.

Many of our leaders down the ages treated this error with levity and cold complicity, and that is why it has continued to ravage the nation. Except for the few arrests, detentions, and the release of a fraction of corrupt men and women in high places, their fight against indiscipline and corruption has yielded no good result. The slim success of arrests and temporary detention of these men of error can never solve the problem of our dear fatherland. After all, after their brief detention and must release, they go back to squander their loot from the nation's treasury. That is why they can afford to roll out drums and organize welcome parties and church thanksgiving services.

If they are thoroughly disciplined according to the law, and their loot and ill-gotten wealth seized, I believe that only a few repentant ones may have cause to shout "Praise the Lord!" President Saul was able to shout "Praise the Lord" because the loot of Amalek operation was stored at the presidential villa. The Lagos ex-convict that celebrated with his party was able to shout "Praise the Lord" because he perhaps still had his loot intact even though the leadership of his day might have told us that the funds were seized. Who in this blessed land confirms such claims? For Saul, the Bible says,

"Samuel was angry when he heard this...He got up early in the morning to confront Saul but was told, 'Saul's gone. He went to Carmel to set up a victory monument in his own honor, and then was headed for Gilgal.' By the time Samuel caught up with him, Saul had just finished an act of sacrifice to God" (15 vs. 11-12 TM)

Just imagine that – adding insult to injury! First, he went to set up a victory monument in his own honor before heading for Gilgal to give God His. Did you see that? Self-importance – giving honor to self while making God the last to honor. Second, he used the accursed things from Amalek to offer burnt offerings or sacrifice to God. What an insult and a slap on Jehovah's face!

Did God receive it? Did God smell the sacrifice? Does God eat meat? The one answer is a total NO! God does not eat meat so it was His Excellency and his party that ate the meat. It was another gala night, or welcome-home party, or another *owambe* organized by the PDGP in honor of Mr. President and to congratulate one another on the success of yet another abuse of opportunity. God help His people!

The constitution of his country, which is, the Law of Moses, provided that every sacrifice by fire that would be acceptable to God must first be clean, blemish-free, and must then be a sweet-smelling sacrifice. It's an offering that God would smell and savor its aroma before the people could eat the roasted flesh. What makes such sacrifices sweet-smelling is the heart that offers it; it must come from a clean heart full of righteousness.

But the Amalek spoil and plunder that Mr. President used to offer burnt sacrifice to God was not only unclean, but it was placed under a curse to be destroyed. So he and his party only made matters worse by offering God and His Parliament accursed things, which were supposed to be totally destroyed on

Amalek soil. Yet, they offered it from a disobedient heart that undermined the holiness of God! And because he took and brought them into the presidential villa, that is, into his government and administration, his presidency was destroyed along with them! How? History tells us,

"Then Samuel said, Do you think all God wants are sacrifices – empty rituals for show? He wants you to listen to him! Plain listening is the thing, not staging a lavish religious production. Not doing what God tells you is far worse than fooling around in the occult. Getting self-important around God is far worse than making deals with your dead ancestors. Because you said No to God's command, he says No to your kingship" (15 vs. 22-23 TM)

That is it.

<u>Kingdom Lost. Kingship Gone</u>

The kingdom was taken away, now the kingship is gone too. What was left? Nothing! May God never say No to your kingship! May He never regret making you the head of that government or organization! May He never announce your retirement or replacement while you are just warming up to take charge of that agency, ministry, or organization! May God never say NO to your candidacy! Only one thing can annul these prayers – disobedience to divine instruction.

Any parent, manager or director, politician or preacher, who brings into their house, office, government, or place of worship that which God and His Parliament have rejected should expect the fate of President Saul as due judgment. Corruption is a curse on any organization or nation. Looting the nation's treasury is a curse and it attracts God's anger on any man, his family, and his nation.

The prophet said to him that listening to God and obeying Him were more important than sacrifices. Not listening to Him is far worse than messing around in the occult. God wanted His Excellency, the man He gave the mandate to listen and obey Him, instead he listened to the people – his party of disobedient folks. The people disobeyed the voice of God's prophet when he told them it was wrong to ask for a human government when God and His Parliament were the real government they had.

In spite of their refusal to listen, Heaven's Parliament consented and gave them the government led by President Saul. Then, they felt that it had become customary for them to always have their way; to continue to disobey God, His Parliament, and His spokesman. Even when the president wanted to obey by waiting further for the right jurisdiction to perform the sacrifice, the same folks prevailed on him to take charge and flout the law!

After all, he was their president and they put him there by consensus vote, and it has become a tradition; a doctrine, and nothing would ever happen. Yet, God gave a second chance, endorsed a second term, but His Excellency claimed in self-defense that it was the people, the same people that persuaded him to disobey again.

What kind of a leader are you? And when perhaps he realized that he, not the people, would be held responsible, he rushed out of the villa to greet and bless the man of God. They had taught him that at the villa; that it's one of the rules of the game of politics – disobedience, and nothing would happen; *we dey kampe!* (Meaning "we are in charge") These things happen in our society almost at all levels and in all sectors, and it is absolutely degrading.

You see a situation where a very good man or woman, living a life worthy of emulation, now rises to a position of leadership in a certain environment with a divine mandate, but they begin to be disloyal, disobedient, and arrogant to God-ordained authority. What has happened? Their club, association, union, or political party has taught them to be so. They teach them that unless they take charge and parley with "the people", they are bound to be impeached by a two-third majority or be voted out at the end of their first term.

They may be threatened with blackmails or to be setup with one humiliating scandal or the other, and finally may mess up their entire career. Then you see that man, who once declared his faith in the God that can do all things, begins to dance to that rhythm out of the fear of man that's no match for his God! That was perhaps what they did to Saul. History further reveals,

"Saul defended himself, 'What are you talking about? I did obey God. I did the job God set for me. I brought in King Agag and destroyed the Amalekites under the terms of the holy ban. So the soldiers (or the people) *saved back a few choice sheep and cattle from the holy ban for sacrifice to God at Gilgal – what's wrong with that?"* (15 vs. 20-21 TM) Emphasis added

Well, Your Excellency, get this straight: As long as God is concerned, everything He places restrictions on is to be meticulously avoided. Whatever He cursed must be destroyed. As far as Heaven was concerned, everything connected with that wicked nation, Amalek, was evil, and ought to be destroyed. Now, that is what is wrong with the choice sheep and cattle!

Fellow citizens – leaders and led alike – let us beware of a little leaven which can mess up our entire lives. Any government or leadership – local, state, federal or at any other level – that must succeed must learn to fear God and respect His commands. They must not take His words for granted because no leader has ever escaped the consequences of doing so.

God is wiser than all His creation put together. To trifle with His clear instructions is to court with His fiery judgment. To obey is better than sacrifice. It is better than any seven-point or ten-point agenda for your country. It is better than any transformation, repositioning or re-branding scheme. To listen to what God says and to obey Him is the key to achieving that agenda. And if you do not have that key then the agenda is useless. President Saul disobeyed and thus lost the kingdom and the kingship. Any leader who follows his bad example will definitely bag the same verdict he got from Heaven's Parliament.

He lost the kingdom – the control over the nation – when he considered the people the first time at Gilgal. Now, he has lost the kingship due to a repeat of the error of looking unto the people. Both the kingdom and the kingship are taken away from the man whose emergence to the seat of authority would have made him to totally submit to God. What's more? The search for a new helmsman began – a man to whom the kingdom and the kingship would be given.

This error of Saul explains why so many leaders especially those in delicate sectors have continued to fall from grace. When they were nobodies, they listened to and obeyed God and His prophets, and God made them heroes. But when they have made it, and have been well established, they no longer listen. They begin to claim that either one godfather somewhere made them or that they are self-made. Therefore, to listen to God and to take instructions from His prophets become secondary issues. They and their godfathers then become more important.

As this unhealthy development goes on, suddenly, they are thrown down from their exalted positions and the deceitful reputation they worked so hard to build and protect is dragged in the mud. Reputation without character is outrageous nonsense!

A thorough look at our key economic and political sectors would reveal how the mighty have been falling. So many bank chiefs and directors in recent times had fallen to the axe of EFCC. Some of them were prosecuted and jailed for sundry financial and criminal offences. Some of these great people who had provided inspiration to the younger generation fell from grace and height because they threw discipline to dogs and right living to the winds; taking the laws into their own hands and misappropriated public funds that ran into billions of naira. Simply put: They moved against the sacred codes that established their privileged positions just as President Saul did, and thus they were thrown out, their associates and subordinates taking over the saddle.

...In Retrospect

If we probe very carefully, the major factor responsible for their greed and subsequent betrayal of public trust is not far from the people who, in one way or another, sponsored their banks' capitalization and consolidation during that era, and also their rise to the apex seats in their organizations. These sponsors might have told them not to worry about breaching the law; that they owned the country and ran things in government – *nothing dey happen* (meaning 'Nothing will happen').

But when, all of a sudden, a Mallam Sanusi, a man who dared the dreaded National Assembly resumed office as the big boss of the Central Bank of Nigeria, the errors of those bank chiefs and their godfathers could not be concealed for long. And the award they earned for themselves from the Silverbird Man of the Year Award winner 2010 was public humiliation. It was a distasteful but quite due and deserving prize for greed.

President Saul tried to defend himself just as some of these our great people tried to defend their dishonorable acts but he was not spared. Just like him, those who tried to defend themselves and explain why they were caught in the spider's web did not succeed as the web holding them was too strong making it easy for the eagle-eyed agency to feast on them.

For the major character we are talking about, no matter how hard he tried; despite the strong appeal by his party to the Highest Authority with their sacrifice at Gilgal, Heaven's Parliament that endorsed him from the beginning, rejected him and threw out the appeal. No matter how any erring leader may try to get off the hook, the long arm of the law that they contravene mindlessly will always catch up and arrest them, and Nemesis will finish the work.

Today, they may retain the kingship after losing the kingdom, but it will not be long the kingship will certainly be taken away from them if they continue to ignore the several calls for change. Although President Saul owned up, yet he did not get off the hook. Yes, he was not let off the hook; the judgment against him was not reversed.

"Saul gave in and confessed, 'I've sinned. I've trampled roughshod over God's word and your (Samuel's) **instruction. I cared more about pleasing the people** (my party)**. I let them tell me what to do. Oh, absolve me of my sin! Take my hand and lead me to the altar so I can worship God!' But Samuel refused: 'No, I can not come alongside you in this. You rejected God's command. Now**

GOD has rejected you as king over Israel'" (15 vs. 24-26 TM) Emphasis mine

Too late to get a nod of collaboration from the prophet on whose shoulder and in whose hands lie his destiny and calling as a king. It was too late to give God an acceptable worship and sacrifice because God has rejected him.

When God rejects a man, it is no use going to the altar to worship because such worship will not be welcomed. This is a very salient piece of truth so many prophets and priests are yet to grasp, and even those who understand it fail to tell it to these men of error so that they do not lose their offerings and substance for the sacrifice. That is why so many of them would tell the culprit not to worry: "Go ahead and bring your sacrificial or worship offerings to the altar, and we will go to God on your behalf, He is a merciful God."

Some of them would make sure His Excellency gives his best for the worship so that God can change his mind. Prophet Balaam did that with President Balak of Moab who provided bulls and rams for sacrifice and God was not happy with the prophet. In the end history recorded this about him,

"They have gone off the road and become lost like Balaam, the son of Beor, who fell in love with money he could make by doing wrong; but Balaam was stopped

from his mad course when his donkey spoke to him with a human voice, scolding and rebuking him" (II Pet. 2 vs. 15-16 TM)

History repeats itself; therefore, what happened to Balaam in the end will befall many who, like him, are running after the wages of unrighteousness.

But Samuel stood his ground and said, **"No, I can not come alongside you in this."** But not so with some of our 21st century prophets who, unfortunately, have been offering strange sacrifices, like Nadab and Abihu, sons of Aaron, upon God's altar. The book of proverbs says, **"The sacrifice of the wicked is an abomination to the LORD: but the prayer of the upright is his delight."**

His Excellency desecrated the altar, how then could he worship there? Unintelligent heroes! Many of our leaders at various levels across the society have desecrated the holy place but are still being led to the altar for worship by some insensitive priests and prophets. For a Samuel who knows that such pious act is borne out of hypocrisy and not out of genuine repentance, they will always refuse to go along.

Suffice it to say that the priest that led the ruling party's chieftain that was released from prison to the altar of partying instead of the altar of penitence was not a priest like Samuel. The priest would have led him first to Gilgal to roll away the reproach and blemish of corruption before leading him to Bethel for re-dedication and quality worship and thanksgiving. A thanksgiving service for his release from prison and a dining and wining session were uncalled for if truly they were thinking like Samuel. This is our submission. We need more Prophet Samuels in our country and our continent than Israel of old needed. I mean the Samuels who would refuse to go alongside hypocrites and lawbreakers to the altar in the name of worship only for them to go back to their filth.

This country is in dire need of men like Samuel who would confront the disobedience of the people and their erring leaders, and lead them to the altar of total repentance from their errors before their sacrifices on the altar of worship would be honored and welcomed by God.

Although President Saul gave in and confessed his sin of favoring the people and letting himself become a puppet-leader, it was however too late to recover the lost kingdom and the kingship. Thus, the tribe of Benjamin from the south lost the presidency and Heaven's Parliament dissolved the People's Disobedience to God Party, PDGP with their manifesto. The kingdom with its kingship returned to the tribe of Judah also in the south.

For those who do not understand the origin of the presidency of God's own country, history is clear on this. Jacob, also known as Israel, zoned the presidency to Judah till Shiloh comes. But when the leaders of Judah and their people disobeyed God, they became slaves and servants to other nations – the act of God. So the only guarantee for Judah in the south to regain and retain the presidency was for her leaders and heroes to continue to obey God.

Like Judah, Nigeria, as God's own state, the giant of Africa and the pride of Jehovah, has also suffered similar fate. It started out same way until our leaders began to let "the people", that is, the godfathers and party chiefs tell them what to do. Then the kingdom and the kingship were never established under them. Then, the government by force only made things worse, and therefore, well-meaning citizens began to call for the abolition of that leadership by force and brute.

But when that call was made, our then leaders – the Generals – wanted, by all means to continue to hold on to the reins of power by succeeding themselves. They wanted to put off the Khaki and put on the *Agbada* and *Babariga* in the name of transition to civil rule. But God stopped them. God and His Parliament stopped them because they did not understand the true meaning of "transition".

Transition connotes death and resurrection which implies the death of brutality, tyranny, callousness, and massive irregularities that characterized both their lives and their governments. Transition also implies the raising of a new life of love for fatherland, oneness, equality, tranquility, and respect for the rule of law, and of course, not leaving out the fear of God.

After about a decade-plus of our democracy, we may have just begun to realize the ideals of true governance with the election of Dr. Goodluck Jonathan from the South-south. No thanks to his political party anyway. In my candid view and in the view of many well-meaning non-partisan political minds, the political party on which Dr. Goodluck Jonathan emerged as President, Commander in Chief of the Armed Forces of the Federal Republic of Nigeria has not done well in delivering on the promises they made to the country in 1998 and 1999.

The reason for that disappointment and their dismal failure is not in the choice of Dr. Goodluck or his predecessors but that there is a crack in their foundation. It was a political movement formed by some of those whose legacies during their years of "active service" to the nation in the first and second republics remain the bane of stagnation of the nation. It is a party formed on a foundation of the "old leaven".

But God decided to graft in the man Jonathan who, perhaps, was not part of that foundation and breed.

In a dramatic but divine way, God pushed him up to the top by stirring the hearts of all the people including members of the opposition parties to vote him in, thus establishing his kingship and the kingdom under him. That over 1.2 million people in the South-west state of Lagos, the seat of the main opposition party cast their votes, their faith and lots for Dr. Goodluck Jonathan simply indicated a divine endorsement and establishment. Another salient fact is: they voted for the man and not for his party!

So then, what could be the expectations of Heaven's Parliament that endorsed him? What could they expect from the people whose hearts and minds they stirred up to accept the man they endorsed as Mr. President? It is very important we get answers to these questions because it will help us to appreciate the great opportunity we have to escape the question, "What hast thou done?" It will also help us to position ourselves for the congratulatory "Well done!"

<u>Plain Listening: The Way Out</u>

The leader should listen to and obey the voice of God and His Parliament while the people should encourage their leader to do so. The people should encourage their leaders to follow the instructions and directions as enshrined in the constitution of the sovereign state – not the sections that favor them, but every section that promotes national interest and Heaven's interest.

Any political party that may produce Mr. President should be willing to allow him as the most senior civil servant of the nation to follow due process of the accepted law in the discharge of his sacred duties. For the current ruling party that has not lived up to expectation, they should work hard to remedy the already woeful condition of the nation which their leadership has not done enough to address since 1999.

As a prophet of God, like Apostle Paul, I speak to their shame. Let the ruling party give this country something good to cheer and shout about. Being the largest political movement in the continent of Africa is not enough: they have to let their bigness reflect on the economies of this God-blessed country and of other African nations that have been staggering and stagnant.

Opposition parties are not spared here; it is their opportunity to fathom out ways to check the counter-productive ways that the current system has birthed. The population has been on the rise; let them make the economy rise too to meet the expectation of the rising populace. The lessons from the error of the biblical

PDGP must be learnt if progress must be recorded in our lands.

Our leaders must first listen to and obey God before considering the people who God used to make their election sure. They must first find out what the Heaven's Parliament would want them to do before looking at any two-third majority decision of the House. This is not to undermine the law that established the House but even Heaven knows that most of the people in those Houses pitch with the decisions that favor their bigotry rather than those that favor the constituencies they represent. This is not an assertion; the lives of the average citizens reflect the exact leadership of the leaders! I write from Heaven's Parliament perspective. Jesus Christ said,

"But I pass no judgment without consulting the Father. I judge as I am told. And my judgment is absolutely fair and just, for it is according to the will of God who sent me and is not merely my own" (John 5 vs. 30 TLB)

Read the Gospels. In other words, "As I see, I talk and write, and what I say is true." These things must be done so that the confession of President Saul and his unpleasant experiences, encounters, and woeful end would not be repeated in our dear heroes and countrymen.

However, we must note that the traits of disappointment and failure that have been obvious in the ruling party from the beginning have not changed. As we express our fear though and note the obvious, we however expect to see drastic positive changes that can ignite our hope and confidence in the various leadership levels across the country which we believe God gave us.

Even though we know from experience now that giving counsel to a group of folks who probably believe they are gods to others and so have the final say could be an effort in futility, yet we cannot afford not to give wise counsel as God puts it in our hearts and mouths. The PDGP of Saul's time did not listen to Prophet Samuel and to God, but we expect that the ruling parties of our time with their leaders should listen to this voice speaking on behalf of God and Heaven's Parliament.

As we round off this volume in our series, our last line is that our dear leaders and their people must choose wisely who to obey and serve. President Saul had a choice between God and his party, but he chose wrongly which he confessed to. In his public confession as chronicled in the Holy Bible, he admitted that he allowed the people, that is, his party, to tell him what to do.

The party's manifesto which was full of self-centered agenda became more important than the sacred manifesto of Heaven's Parliament which centered on empowering, enriching, and exalting the people of God from squalor to stardom, and from the pit of frustration and retrogression to the palace of fulfilment and celebration. God's manifesto, no matter how the most intelligent and most intellectual minds view and regard it, remains the only source and guarantee for the people's manifestation of greatness.

Saul ignored it by the counsel of his party, and he ended up losing his kingship and the kingdom. If our presidents, governors, lawmakers, heads of ministries, departments and agencies, royal fathers, clergy etc., ignore God's manifesto for His people, they will doubtless end like Saul Kish.

I know what it means to be a leader over a people. Irrespective of the population and the level of leadership, leadership is leadership. If a councilor does not perform well in his ward, he may not even perform well when he is given a local government area to oversee

I was once a youth president in one of the big churches in Lagos. When, in 2005, the senior pastor told me that I was going to take over from my predecessor, I was not particularly excited because I had been serving in acting capacity for about three years before that time. Then, he wanted to choose a vice for me but I told him to allow me prayerfully choose my assistant. Thank God he consented to my request.

And you know what; all the people that he suggested I should consider for the office of a vice president of the youth ministry did not even stay long after my appointment – God's design. They were big boys who probably mused, "How could Chris lead us?" Hmm...Good question.

As the youth president at that mission's area headquarters with other youth leaders of other branches of the mission looking up to me, I severally found myself in situations where I must choose from a set of options. Sometimes, I had to choose between listening to and obeying the two "camps" that, as it were, validated my appointment – the pastorate and the people (the youths).

If the youths had said NO to my appointment as their president, the pastorate would have had no choice but to look for another candidate. And even if they had pushed against the will of those youths to install me, it would have been a herculean task for me to perform my duties because some of those youths were no easy nuts to crack back then.

But since they saw my appointment as a welcome development, they also expected me to listen to them just as the pastorate expected me to listen to them. However, I had to do what was right and good even though sometimes it attracted applause and commendations from one camp and disapproval and condemnation from the other.

I remember that one of my former cabinet members, a very good friend from the time I was the acting president, once confronted me: "Obigwe, you appoint into the cabinet youths who are loyal to you and who would not challenge your leadership." And I replied him, "I choose potential leaders who understand what leadership means and what it takes to support a man of visions and who would not challenge decisions made for the progress and in the interest of the mission." The question now is: Did I succeed in that capacity? Yes, I did, and that, they would hardly forget.

Now if you think it was easy because it was in a religious assembly, think again. Presidency is presidency – and I can tell you of the politicking that goes on even in a small group in a religious assembly. After all, in a religious assembly, you find people of different schools of thought and backgrounds such that managing them is not as easy as one might think. In fact, it is easier to lead a corporate or business organization than to lead a religious group because there, the employer pays the employee as long as both parties keep their agreement. Remember, the man who pays the piper dictates the tone.

But it is not so in a religious assembly where you pay only a few staff. In a religious house, it is your credibility and integrity that can buy the members allegiance. If you cannot manage a department in a company, who would make you a general manager of the company? If you cannot successfully lead a department in a Church, truth is, you are not likely to succeed as a senior pastor or a general overseer of a mission. Do remember that Jesus said, ***"He that is faithful in little shall be faithful in much."*** I am not trying to sound too self-important here; I am just stating the obvious; yes, the truth.

So if you cannot account for your stewardship as a ward councilor or a community head, then you cannot survive the storm as Mr. President. One of my mentors, Pastor Olumide Emmanuel always tells us that new levels attract new devils! And I believe him. It is self-explanatory. So let our excellences and royalties do what is right and good before God for their people, and not only for themselves.

To make a choice between men of power and God of power has never been an easy thing to do. You see and feel these men – their commendations and applause, diplomacies and politicking, threats and blackmails –

but you only see and feel God with the eye and mind of faith; He does not come around your office as men of power do. So that makes it easy to fall prey to the men you see and feel and know their penchant for making refuters suffer the consequence. But you do not think God would do like them; He is the good gentleman that understands, you know the popular line down here: "God understands" even when you did not hear Him say so. Our presumptions! Our assumptions! Our doom! But the experience of President Saul and his People's Disobedience to God Party (PDGP) should serve as a veritable guide.

Our wise counsel again is that leaders should listen to the God of power whose interest is for the goodwill of the people; that righteousness, justice and equity may prevail in the land! If Saul had listened to and obeyed God and Samuel, both the kingdom and his kingship would have been firmly established in his country by the God of all power and all dominion. Even though he confessed to failing God and disappointing the prophet, the judgment stayed – his replacement was sought, found, endorsed, and anointed while he was still on the throne without power!

History revealed that immediately the new president-elect was anointed to take over the kingship and the kingdom, the Spirit of God left Saul and in its place, an evil spirit was released to torment and trouble him. The

Spirit of repentance towards God; the Spirit of excellence and godliness, of truth and faithfulness left him while the spirit of permanent error possessed him. That was why he began to hunt down anyone who did right in the sight of God and the people. He even sought ways to eliminate his successor-elect, and anyone who pledged allegiance to David was in trouble. He resorted to witch-hunting; practiced witchcraft and patronized witches in secret.

And where did all these lead him to? They led him far away from Gilgal where he was first commissioned as president and commander in chief to Gilboa where he was finally conquered and ended up dead. President Saul, his sons, many of his soldiers and his PDGP chieftains died shamefully on the mount of Gilboa in the hands of the greatest opposition of their lives and their government. They never lived to tell the story of defeat or conquest; the oppositions and challenges they set out to fight swallowed them up and lived on.

Our dear heroes, where did you start? And where will you end? Think. How did you start? And how will you end? Again, think. O! How I pray that our contemporary heroes and leaders will learn the brazen lessons from these ones that fell and let God, not "the people", play the tune and rhythm to which they would dance.

May God help our heroes to avoid and even now correct the error of Saul and the People's Disobedience to God Party in order to avert what is coming – a tragic end! Did you say, amen? You had better because a tragic end is brewing, and only the wise and prudent will escape it. But like my great political editor, Uzonna Ononye would say, Time will tell!

FINALLY...

A SHOT AS I SEE IT

"If I have seen farther than others, it is because I have stood on the shoulders of giants"- NEWTON

Let me begin this last lap by thanking you for your patience to read through the entire chapters of this book. I admit from this end that it is no little sacrifice you have made. It shows that you truly understand what it means to be virtuous and patriotic in a time when many who claim so only pay lip-service and live a lie. Most importantly, I commend you, I mean you, who have received a kind of spanking by the hard truths unveiled in this book especially you that was once a hero but somehow found yourself in errors.

However, the only one thing that would prompt and move your generation to recognize my commendation of you and consequently celebrate you is your decision now to get back on track; put an end to the errors, and become a great patriot and ambassador you were made to be. This means that my commendation of your patience and understanding without the people's recognition of your active patriotism may not earn you the unanimous voice that you deserve in order to be celebrated. After all, a life void of celebration is as empty as a drum in the harmattan.

Now, it will not be complete if I do not point out some issues the way they should be. These are things that should complement the issues already written in previous chapters. ***"No one can receive anything unless it is given to him from heaven"*** (John 3:27).

In September 2009, I received the title of this book in what seemed like a trance. Then, I had realized that the errors of our past heroes had pursued, overtaken, and overwhelmed their labors. But I had practically forgot about that experience until January 2011 when life's unpredictable experiences forced me into a "prison life" – a kind of an Island of Patmos where my eyes were opened to understand why it was so and why I should write on this title.

Now when I say "prison life", I do not mean that I was imprisoned but that I was living like someone who was in prison. I had no house at that time; my pregnant wife with our first child was taking refuge at her parents' house while I was hanging out with a married couple who had no child at the time. No business was coming and so no money to spend. And to make matters worse and unfortunate, my friends and many who claimed to love me were nowhere to be found. Then, the Lord instructed me not to beg for any help from anybody although I disobeyed few times but never got anything from them. That was when I knew that I was at my Island of Patmos!

When John wrote the Revelations of the Holy Bible, he gave a shot as he saw it. All the prophets of God who ever lived gave the shots as they saw them. For me, I have given the shot as was revealed to me the way I saw it. Yet, I have much more to say on the errors of our heroes and will not hesitate to do so if God permits me.

Let no leader occupying any office at home, school, church, mosque, office, bank, private and public institutions take this for granted. This is because those who did so to the prophets of old never lived to tell their experiences instead others wrote about them. I can confidently share with you one of the several encounters I had as soon as I began writing this book by divine direction. It is a revelation that is still fresh on my mind and the sight so clear even when I close my eyes.

It was about 4:30a.m, Saturday 19th February, 2011 exactly six weeks from the day the LORD tapped me in the night and said, "Son, get up and write" even though I did not know how or where to start or even the exact things to write.

In the spirit, I saw myself in a village hall meeting with some elderly men and a few other men in their 50s who looked artificially older than they were. All of them were dressed in traditional attires and were sitting on long wooden benches. I was the only one sitting alone on the last bench at the back row, but then I was wearing a modern-day western attire – a shirt and a pair of trousers to be exact.

Someone that looked like Dr. Goodluck Jonathan, but much older than he is at press time, stood in front of the seated audience and addressed them. He was actually taking the opinions of the rest of the people who appeared to be disturbed by the state of the nation.

Just then, the late Pa Anthony Enahoro stood up and spoke. I recognized him immediately but could not get what he said because I was greatly overwhelmed and was lost in thought as I recognized and admired the late Dr. Nnamdi Azikiwe sitting next to him right before me. Pa Enahoro finished talking and sat down. I then tapped him and asked him what he had said. He turned and looked at me, just realizing that I was sitting behind him all the while though did not know who I was, and he replied, "How can we make progress when we have failed to acknowledge our problem?" These were not his exact words but that was what I could get from his reply as I was still amazed and wondering how privileged I was to be in such a meeting and to meet such heroes I had only seen on the television screen and on pages of newspapers.

However, disappointment and regret were clearly written on his face and on the face of Dr. Nnamdi

Azikiwe. They looked very unhappy but the reasons for their unhappiness, they did not tell me. In fact, Dr. Azikiwe made no comment in the meeting; however, the sad expression on his face gave me a clue. The state of Nigerian and African states made him very sad.

Then as I straightened up to listen to the moderator, a much older Goodluck Jonathan, as he gave a concluding remark, Dr. Nnamdi Azikiwe turned back and looked long at me but still said nothing. The expression on his face was clear enough and the message it carried was well understood by me. It hit me when I realized how disappointed he was and how he had wished to see things better if it was possible for him to take the podium once again. Then, being moved by his worried look, I tapped him on his right shoulder with my left hand and assured him that everything would be fine. It was a long meeting. I had even thought it was in real life until I was brought back to this realm from my sleep. It was one encounter that I would never forget in my entire life!

Now do not forget: nothing in the spirit realm happens by accident. In fact, if you would take this rare truth: nothing of this sort happens by accident – there are no accidents. Furthermore, this goes to buttress my earlier point that God is as much interested in this beautiful country as He was in Israel of old times. Truth is: God runs this Universe, He created it, manages it and therefore, He is so much interested in how things turn out in every part of it.

This country and the African continent have seen so much peril for a long time courtesy of the terrible errors of our leaders, and cannot afford to continue in that negative trend any longer. Even though it appears unattainable at the moment due to the fact that the mountain created by the massive corruption that has eaten deep into our system looks insurmountable, yet we all should not give in to apathy.

Every well-meaning citizen of this country and the people of this continent should have a sober reflection, quit their lives of errors, and put God first in all of their endeavors. Those who, like Saul, have brushed God aside and betrayed divine appointment by reverencing the people must go back to Gilgal and get it right in order to avoid ending up in disgrace and dishonor at Gilboa. God must come first and the God-factor must take the centre of our existence. Finally, all these they must do bearing in mind that the Supreme Ruler of the ends of the Earth and Governor among the Nations – GOD ALMIGHTY will call them to account for every of their deeds or actions.

The most important feature or characteristic of a hero worthy of commendation and celebration is self-sacrifice. The ability and willingness to sacrifice personal comfort for the comfort of others makes a leader outstanding, humble, resourceful, tolerant, and successful. To sacrifice personal gains will translate to reducing and relieving the people of needless pains. Self-sacrifice makes a leader corrupt-free because he no longer thinks of what to get for himself but what to give to others. He sees public office as an avenue to make positive monumental impact on the people while leaving a legacy of selfless service for coming generations. Nigerian and indeed African leadership must graduate from their present level of selfishness to that desirable and commendable life of self-sacrifice.

To become a true hero means to come, see, fight, and conquer. Some came but failed to see and so could not fight or conquer. Some have come and have seen, but either lacked the capacity and ability to fight and conquer, or they simply failed to fight. Yet others have come, have seen, and have engaged in the fight against the odds that have kept our world in darkness but could not conquer. Their failure to conquer was either because they leaned on their own understanding and strength, or they allowed themselves to be overpowered by the odds they fought against. However, only a few others seem to be conquering, but their conquest has had little impact on their environment.

In the land of the blind where the only one-eyed man is crowned king, the lives of the people who are blind would remain miserable no matter how hard their one-eyed king fights to make them comfortable. The only way they can become truly liberated and live comfortably is when they all have their sights restored, otherwise no level of comfort that's provided for them would be of value when they cannot see it and appreciate it.

Similarly, no amount of preaching given to a hungry man that food would soon be ready would suffice when he has not been asked what kind of food he would like to eat. Otherwise the cook ends up preparing what the hungry man regards as poison. This is because one man's food is another's poison.

Everyone in the position of leadership is actually a servant; a minister and they are required to find out what the people they're serving really need before providing it. Everybody wants good life and if their leaders can give it to them, they will be alright. God saw that in all of mankind's desperation they needed salvation, and He provided it even when they were not qualified for it.

"Christ arrives right on time ... He did not, and doesn't, wait for us to get ready. He presented himself for this sacrificial death when we were far too weak and

rebellious to do anything to get ourselves ready. And even if we hadn't been so weak, we would not have known what to do anyway. We can understand someone dying for a person worth dying for, and we can understand how someone good and noble could inspire us to selfless sacrifice. But God put his love on the line for us by offering his Son in sacrificial death while we were of no use whatever to him" (Romans 5:6-8 TM)

Did you get the last line there? *"...while we were of no use to him"* He showed us love. Now, that is what it means to be a true leader – a hero. God was – and remains – focused and He achieved His plans. So, every true leader must do the same if they must achieve their God-talks.

Corruption is a distraction that must be avoided with tenacity and the fear of God in order to focus on the great task of making good people and building a great nation. No excuse is genuine for failure. **"A hunter who has only one arrow must not shoot with careless aim"** (African Proverb). This is the shot as I see it.

ABOUT THE AUTHOR

Christogonus Leo is a multi-graced minister of God. A graduate of the Redeemed Christian Bible College (R.C.B.C.) and of the School of Disciples (SOD) both in Lagos, Nigeria, Chris is also a minister in songs and drama, a versatile master of ceremonies, an eloquent motivational speaker, and a music artiste with a touch of distinction and class.

The Professor, as he's fondly addressed by his friends, impacts the lives of many young people of his community through several quality and destiny-shaping programs he initiates within and outside the community of believers.

For example, in 2005, Chris organized a talent hunt program tagged Youth Talent Showcase 2005 which was supported by some mega companies in Nigeria. In 2006, he initiated and convened a youth conference which he tagged Youth Conference 2006 with the theme "Youths As Instruments of Change In The Next Democratic Dispensation". This conference had Barrister Wale Ogunade – a human rights lawyer as chief guest speaker plus a few other speakers. Amongst the special guests who were invited to the conference was Mr. Opeyemi Bamidele – the then Commissioner for Youths, Sports, and Social Development of Lagos State.

The conference which was organized to sensitize and prepare the youths in the community ahead of the 2007 general elections in Nigeria drew the attention and presence of men of the press from some newspaper houses, and was covered by the Nigerian Television Authority (NTA) Lagos.

Pastor Chris speaks at conferences and conventions addressing a wide range of issues that affect the society and the community of believers. He is the author of several books including the series, The Errors of our Heroes Past, Volumes 1-5. He is married and blessed with children.

REFERENCES

Written by inspiration of God between January 2011 and January 2012

First Published on www.amazon.com/kdp **under International Copyright Laws, August 2017**

All scripture quotations are from the Holy Bible: Authorized Kings James Version (KJV) Red Letter Edition.

Verses marked TLB are taken from The Living Bible, copyright@1971. Used by permission of Tyndale House Publishers, Inc. Wheaton, Illinois 60189. All rights reserved.

Verses marked (TM) are taken from The Message, copyright@ 1993, 1994, 1995, 1996, 2000, 2001, 2002. Eugene Peterson - The Message Bible

Punch Newspapers Friday November 19, 2010

Punch Newspapers Friday November 26, 2010

Sunday Champion November 14, 2010

Punch Newspapers Monday January 10, 2011

Punch Newspapers Thursday February 17, 2011

ThisDay Newspapers Saturday July 23, 2011

Bob Gass - The Word for Today

Longman Dictionary of Contemporary English 6th Edition

Special Credits

Uche Igwe

Joseph Adeyeye

Anyiam Osigwe

Dele Momodu

Abimbola Adelakun

Ben Nanaghan

Ezekiel Ette

Emmanuel Nwachukwu

Gbenga Adeniji, and others whose names could not appear in this book, thank you for your inspirations.